PAM 700-16: The Army Ammunition Management System

United States Department of the Army

Department of the Army
Pamphlet 700–16

LOGISTICS

THE ARMY AMMUNITION MANAGEMENT SYSTEM

Headquarters
Department of the Army
Washington, DC
1 December 1982

SUMMARY of CHANGE

DA PAM 700-16
THE ARMY AMMUNITION MANAGEMENT SYSTEM

Not applicable.

o

o

Headquarters
Department of the Army
Washington, DC
1 December 1982

*Department of the Army
Pamphlet 700–16

LOGISTICS

THE ARMY AMMUNITION MANAGEMENT SYSTEM

By Order of the Secretary of the Army:

E. C. MEYER
General, United States Army
Chief of Staff

Official:

ROBERT M. JOYCE
Major General, United States Army
The Adjutant General

History. This publication has been organized to make it compatible with the Army electronic publishing database. No content has been changed.

Summary. This publication provides a system description for management of the ammunition program by the Department of the Army. It is intended to be a relatively stable document; however, revisions will be published as required for accuracy and currency. As a companion document, the Army Ammunition Plan will be published during the third quarter of the fiscal year to provide composite information which reflects the fiscal support for ammunition in the POM process. The Army Ammunition Plan will reflect the time-oriented planning of the DA Staff and major Army commands for achieving the Army goals in ammunition development, production, procurement, storage, maintenance, supply, and distribution.

Applicability. This document is the system description directed by the Chief of Staff. It is intended to furnish a qualitative conceptual framework for integration of all Department of the Army activities in support of providing ammunition to United States operational forces and foreign military forces under security assistance programs. This includes ammunition research, development, and acquisition; distribution, storage, and maintenance; and ammunition production base readiness, modernization, and expansion.

Proponent and exception authority. The proponent agency of this pamphlet is the Office of the Deputy Chief of Staff for Research, Development, and Acquisition.

Interim changes. Users of this pamphlet will not implement interim changes unless the change document has been authenticated by The Adjutant General. If a formal printed change is not received by the time the interim change expires, users will destroy the interim change.

Suggested Improvements. Users are invited to send comments and suggested improvements on DA Form 2028 (Recommended Changes to Publications and Blank Forms) directly to HQDA (DAMA–CSM–M) WASH DC 20310.

Distribution. *Active Army, ARNG, USAR:* To be distributed in accordance with DA Form 12–9A requirements for DA Pamphlets Logistics and Logistics Plans—D.

Contents (Listed by paragraph and page number)

---

*This pamphlet supersedes DA Pam 700–16, dated 15 February, 1979.

UNCLASSIFIED

Contents—Continued

Contents—Continued

Glossary

RESERVED

Chapter 1
INTRODUCTION

1-1. Background and authority.

a. In response to a Chief of Staff directive, the Army Staff undertook a major effort to enhance the overall ammunition posture of Army forces identified for NATO deployment in the FY77 timeframe. This effort created an awareness of need for overall coordination of individual functional activities relating to ammunition.

b. In recognition of this need, a Chief of Staff directive designated the Deputy Chief of Staff for Research, Development, and Acquisition (DCSRDA) as the principal Army Staff ammunition management executive, with authority for integration and coordination of Army Staff efforts to increase the effectiveness of the Army's management of the ammunition life cycle. The DCSRDA was further charged to—

(1) Establish and maintain a detailed system description of the ammunition life cycle process describing the interfaces of the commands/agencies involved and developing time schedules for the accomplishment of major objectives in the ammunition integrated management system.

(2) Initiate changes to the system as optimization studies may dictate.

c. The Chief of Staff had also directed a follow-on planning effort to provide distribution combat rates, theater requirements, stockage and storage objectives, construction requirements, and procurement programs for all theaters in the FY79, 83, and 86 timeframes. The DCSRDA also became responsible for this follow-on plan.

d. Recognition, in 1976, of markedly higher combat consumption rates for NATO-deployed forces also brought with it recognition of need for improvements in intratheater handling and distribution of ammunition. This awakening has in turn spawned other initiatives to enhance the Army's conventional ammunition postures. These are discussed in the following paragraphs individually. The most important of these ongoing activities is the implementation of the comprehensive DAIG Conventional Ammunition Special Review (CASPR) Report's recommendations.

e. The CASPR was an in-depth review of conventional ammunition, worldwide, conducted by The Inspector General (TIG). The report was accepted by the CSA in August 1980, and addressed all major issues, including organization for management, life cycle phases, acquisition, operational aspects, logistical functions, and readiness implications. The report identified 109 major recommendations for improvement of the Army's (Conventional) Ammunition Management System. The DCSRDA was assigned responsibility for implementation of the CASPR Report. A management strategy for accomplishing this tasking has been developed and status is being provided via a CASPR General Officer Steering Committee, VCSA IPR, Army Ammunition Plan, and the HQDA Quarterly Ammunition Review (QAR). The CASPR Report represents the Army's ongoing effort to improve the conventional ammunition system.

f. The Ammunition Initiatives Task Force (AITF), formed in response to the Vice Chief of Staff's directive, developed 75 recommendations covering both hardware development and procurement and doctrinal and organizational changes. These recommendations were approved, and the DCSRDA was designated as responsible for monitoring each recommendation and including its status in the Army Ammunition Plan.[1]

g. The Training Ammunition Authorization Committee (TAAC) was established as a continuing standing committee of the Department of the Army. The TAAC, composed of General Officer or equivalent senior Army representatives of interested staff agencies and major commands (MACOMs), is the executive forum established under the chairmanship of the Deputy Chief of Staff for Operations and Plans for the purpose of reviewing Army training ammunition resources, training goals, management procedures, training programs, and related activities.

h. The Training Ammunition Management System[2] (TAMS) was established under the primary Army Staff responsibility of the Deputy Chief of Staff for Operations and Plans. TAMS is the interface with the Army Planning, Programing, and Budgeting System (PPBS) and provides for managerial control of munitions expended in training.

1-2. Purpose.

a. This document is the system description directed by the Chief of Staff. It is intended to furnish a qualitative conceptual framework for integration of all Department of the Army activities in support of providing ammunition to United States operational forces and foreign military forces under security assistance programs. This includes ammunition research, development, and acquisition; distribution, storage, and maintenance; and ammunition production base readiness, modernization, and expansion.

b. The related Army Ammunition Plan provides to the Army major commands and agencies information regarding ammunition and ammunition support that can be expected in the near- to mid-term within current funding constraints. The Army Ammunition Plan consists of a series of interrelated plans in all applicable functional areas.

1-3. Major functions.

a. In addition to the overall executive responsibility previously described, the DCSRDA continues to exercise management of ammunition research, development, and acquisition activities. With regard to agencies and commands

---

[1] AR 15–20, Training Ammunition Authorization Committee, February 1977.

[2] AR 5–13, Training Ammunition Management System, September 1979.

under the cognizance of other DA Staff agencies, the DCSRDA exercises his overall responsibilities through and with the cognizant agency (i.e., for matters pertaining to Military Traffic Management Command (MTMC), in concert with Office, Deputy Chief of Staff for Logistics (ODCSLOG)).

b. The Deputy Chief of Staff for Operations and Plans (DCSOPS) retains authority for the Training Ammunition Management System (TAMS), determination of the force structure to be supported, the ammunition consumption rates, chairs the Training Ammunition Authorization Committee (TAAC), and establishment, where necessary, of priorities for development and distribution. The Deputy Chief of Staff for Logistics (DCSLOG) is responsible for the logistics aspects of Integrated Logistic Support (ILS); management of the fielded conventional ammunition stockpile; and the development of concepts, plans, policies, and procedural guidance for all conventional ammunition logistical missions and functions. The Chief of Engineers retains proponent functions for facilities. Each agency is responsible for keeping ODCSRDA informed of proponent actions influencing the ability of the system to satisfy requirements.

1–4. Organizational elements of the system.

a. Below the level of Headquarters, Department of the Army (HQDA), the major operational elements responsible for accomplishing various aspects of the Army ammunition program are—

(1) *The US Army Materiel Development and Readiness Command (DARCOM).* Subordinate commands and activities of the US Army Materiel Development and Readiness Command (DARCOM), which coordinates the program development and execution of these elements—

(a) *The US Army Armament Materiel Readiness Command (ARRCOM).* Wholesale materiel management, production base support, procurement, and production of Army standardized ammunition and selected, standardized conventional ammunition items of the other services assigned to the Army as the DOD Single Manager for Conventional Ammunition (SMCA).

(b) *Munitions Production Base Modernization Agency (MPBMA) (subordinate activity of ARRCOM).* Management of the Department of Defense (DOD) Munitions Modernization and Expansion Program; Ammunition Facility Design and Procurement; Manufacturing Methods and Technology (MMT); Modernization and Expansion Projects; and Plant Equipment Package modernization.

(c) *US Army Defense Ammunition Center and School (USADACS) (subordinate activity of ARRCOM).* Provision of technical, logistical, consultation, engineering, training, career management, and other specialized services for and in support of class V managers, DARCOM project/product managers, functional managers, major subordinate commands, field service activities, logistic assistance offices, and depots associated with worldwide ammunition logistic functions. This includes management of the Ammunition School; the Ammunition Depot Modernization Program; the Ammunition Civilian Quality Assurance Career Program; the Department of the Army Program for palletization, unitization, transportation, and storage methods for class V ammunition and ammunition peculiar equipment (APE); and the Department of the Army Worldwide Ammunition Logistic Support and Review Program (AR 700–13).

(d) *Central Ammunition Management Office, Pacific (CAMO-PAC) (subordinate activity of ARRCOM).* Central management of all US Army munition stocks within the Pacific; integrates and coordinates requirements and distribution; requisitions all munitions for the Pacific; formulates, monitors, and directs maintenance programs; monitors quality assurance and explosive safety programs; and serves as the Standard Army Ammunition System (SAAS) (see appendix B–4) manager for the Pacific area.

(e) *US Army Armament Research and Development Command (ARRADCOM).* Development and initial acquisition of new items of ammunition; technical support, if required, for fielded ammunition.

(f) *US Army Depot System Command (DESCOM).* CONUS depot storage operations, maintenance, and distribution to and from CONUS depots; distribution plan computations, in coordination with ARRCOM for SMCA assigned items.

(g) *US Army Missile Command (MICOM).* Development, acquisition, and material management of small rockets procured from the ammunition appropriation (PAA-Procurement of Ammunition, Army).

(h) *US Army Test and Evaluation Command (TECOM).* Development, production, and surveillance testing of ammunition.

(i) *US Army Electronics Research and Development Command (USAERADCOM).* Technology base for fluidic and electronic fuzing.

(j) *US Army Materials and Mechanics Research Center (USAMMRC).* Technology base for materials research and basic materials manufacturing processes.

(2) *MTMC.* Subordinate commands and activities of MTMC, which is the DOD Single Manager for intraCONUS and intertheater movement of all commodities, to include ammunition, and provides time-phased Service-developed lift requirements to Military Sealift Command (MSC) and Military Airlift Command (MAC)—

(a) *Eastern Area, MTMC.* Traffic management of ammunition movements, eastern half of CONUS.

(b) *Western Area, MTMC.* Traffic management of ammunition movements, western half of CONUS.

(c) *US Army Terminal Group, Europe.* Ocean terminal operations in support of US Army Europe (USAREUR).

(3) *US Army Europe (USAREUR).*

(a) *Headquarters, USAREUR.* Plans, policy, and programs for logistics support concepts, force structure, facilities, budgeting, positioning of stocks and actions involving other NATO countries.

(b) 200th Theater Army Materiel Management Center (TAMMC) Director of Ammunition Management, USAREUR. Munitions materiel management, storage, maintenance, and distribution for the European Theater.

(4) US Army Japan (USARJ). Munitions materiel management, quality assurance, maintenance, and storage for war reserves in support of Korea plus distribution for the Command.

(5) US Eighth Army (EUSA). Munitions materiel management, quality assurance, storage, and distribution for US Eighth Army and ROK War Reserve Stocks for Allies (WRSA).

(6) US Army Western Command (WESTCOM). Munitions materiel management, quality assurance, storage, and distribution for WESTCOM.

b. Principal supporting Army organizations are—

(1) US Army Training and Doctrine Command (TRADOC). Represents interests of the user; develops doctrine for logistic support; develops statements of materiel requirements; monitors requirements and distribution for TRADOC installations.

(a) US Army Missile and Munitions Center and School (USAMMCS). Combat developments and training to include organization, staffing, equipage, and employment of ammunition units and training of military ammunition personnel.

(2) US Army Forces Command (FORSCOM). Monitors requirements and distribution for FORSCOM installations and organizations.

(3) US Army Operational Test and Evaluation Agency (OTEA). User (operational) testing of development items (Field Operating Agency of Chief of Staff).

(4) US Army Concepts Analysis Agency (CAA). Principal US Army wargaming agency, provides major input to ODCSOPS for ammunition rates computation of requirements in support of the operations and contingency plans (Field Operating Agency of Chief of Staff).

(5) US Army Logistics Evaluation Agency (USALEA). Determination of support requirements and supportability of ammunition items (Field Operating Agency of ODCSLOG).

c. Integration of the functioning of all these elements will occur in the framework of the Army Planning, Programming, and Budgeting System (PPBS). This is the system through which resources are allocated to the various major program elements which support the ammunition program. The PPBS is also the medium for assignment of priorities among Program Elements within the annual Total Obligational Authority (TOA) guidance as specified by the Office of the Secretary of Defense (OSD). The resulting total Army program is then published annually in the POM.

Chapter 2
LIFE CYCLE OF TYPICAL ROUND OF AMMUNITION

2–1. Inception/requirements documentation.

a. The life cycle of a typical round of conventional ammunition is depicted in figure 2–1. The initial concept for development of a new round of ammunition or generic group of munitions (such as the Improved Conventional Munitions "Family") may originate either within the research and development community or within the user community. Perhaps more so in ammunition than in other commodities, a demonstrated potential for improved performance often leads to a formally stated requirement rather than the converse. Generally, "more" equates to "better." The user is interested in ammunition which is more accurate, more lethal, more reliable, lighter weight, less bulky, and which contains insensitive explosive filler, or offers some other quantifiable advantage. Further, drawdowns of existing stocks through combat, training, and testing consumption often offer an opportunity to replace older designs with newer designs, without the trauma associated with obsolescence of a combat vehicle fleet or other major items of capital equipment. Introduction of new items occurs with some frequency and older items are phased out with lesser frequency, keeping the inventory in an almost constant state of change. Change, in the direction of enhanced performance, can bring concomitant penalties. Most current weapons systems are high performance systems, in which even a minute change in one system parameter can have a profound change on system components. For example, attempts to secure higher velocity with state-of-the-art propellants bring with them higher breech pressures and accelerated bore erosion. The operational flexibility common to the use of older, less sophisticated, general-purpose ammunition is sometimes lost upon introduction of more modern but often more specialized ammunition.

b. The Letter of Agreement (LOA) is the normal requirements document used to initiate advanced development of ammunition items, in accordance with Army Regulation (AR) 71–9. The LOA is jointly prepared and authenticated by the materiel (DARCOM) and combat (TRADOC) developers, in coordination with the logistician (USALEA), when they both agree that a materiel concept has sufficient interest, importance, or operational and technical potential to warrant the commitment of advanced development resources to obtain more definitive information. The purpose of the LOA is to ensure agreement between the combat developer and materiel developer on the nature and characteristics of a proposed system and the investigation required to develop and validate the systems concept, and to define associated operational, technical, and logistical support concepts during the conduct of these investigations. The LOA is the document of record to support effort in the system Advanced Development (6.3.b) category of the Research, Development, Test and Evaluation (RDTE) program. Its preparation is initiated during Concept Exploration, and approval authorizes entry into the Demonstration and Validation Phase (para 2–2b(2)).

c. LOAs which project Advanced Development costs in excess of $20 million or later revise advanced development costs to exceed $20 million will be forwarded by the combat developer to HQDA (ODCSOPS) for approval; all other LOAs will be approved at the materiel developer and combat developer level and forwarded to HQDA (ODCSOPS) for information. In unusual circumstances, LOAs not in excess of $20 million may be specifically selected for HQDA decision.

d. The Required Operational Capability (ROC) document is the requirements document used to initiate engineering development of ammunition items. It is prepared by the appropriate TRADOC agency, in coordination with the DARCOM major subordinate command and the logistician (USALEA), and approved by HQDA (ODCSOPS). It is a concise, quantitative statement of the minimum essential operational, technical, training, logistical, and cost information necessary to initiate full-scale engineering development. It is initiated during the Demonstration and Validation Phase and must be approved prior to entering the Full-Scale Engineering Development Phase (para 2-2b(3)).

2–2. Ammunition research and development cycle.

a. New items of ammunition are developed on an event-oriented schedule, as specified in AR 1000–1 and the AR 70 series, with the pacing factor to be work completed, rather than calendar-controlled milestones. The Planning, Programing, and Budgeting System (PPBS) cycle must be taken into account, however, and it is often necessary to budget for RDTE funds in advance of successful attainment of intermediate R&D goals. In these events, obligation of the funds is then deferred pending attainment of the goals and demonstration of readiness to proceed with subsequent phases of the program.

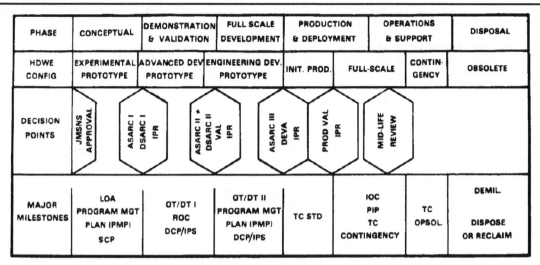

Figure 2-1. Life Cycle of a Typical Round of Conventional Ammunition
* See new DODI 5000.2

b. The R&D cycle is divided into three major phases—

(1) *Conceptual Phase,* in which the technical, military, and economic basis for proposed developmental ammunition systems/items are established and concept formulation initiated through pertinent studies and the development and evaluation of experimental hardware.

(2) *Demonstration and Validation Phase,* in which preliminary design and engineering are verified, tradeoff proposals analyzed, logistics problems identified during the Conceptual Phase resolved or minimized, formal requirement document prepared, and the concept validated for full-scale development.

(3) *Full-Scale Development Phase,* in which engineering is completed, relatively large numbers of the munition are produced in the final design configuration and tested under a wide variety of environmental conditions, and a decision is made on whether the item is acceptable for type classification and follow-on production and deployment.

c. R&D tests are broadly divided into two categories: Development Testing (DT) in accordance with AR 70–10 and Operational Testing (OT) in accordance with AR 71–3. Most of the DT is performed by TECOM. Most of the major OT is performed under the auspices of OTEA, usually by a troop unit of the FORSCOM, in coordination with the proponent TRADOC school (e.g., the Armor Center and School for tank ammunition). Both DT and OT are further divided according to major program phasing as follows:

(1) DT I and OT I are accomplished during the Demonstration and Validation Phase. Upon completion of this phase, an in-process review (IPR) is held to verify the readiness of the item to enter the Full-Scale Development Phase.

(2) DT II and OT II are accomplished during the Full-Scale Development Phase, at the end of which the Development Acceptance IPR is held (for nonmajor systems). At this IPR it may be decided that the item completely meets all established requirements, in which case it is type classified "Standard" and cleared for full-scale production. Alternatively, to provide maximum assurance that the design is suited to hard tooled mass production and, conversely, that the production version exhibits the performance characteristics verified for the design in Full-Scale Development, it may be decided on an exception basis to designate the item "Limited Production" (LP), and clear it only for low-rate production.

(3) In this latter event, testing (DT and/or OT) as directed at the IPR is conducted with low-rate production items. At the conclusion of this test cycle, a Production Validation IPR is held. If the item has met all test objectives, it will be declared "Standard" and cleared for mass production. If this testing had disclosed minor deficiencies in the design or the Technical Data Package (TDP), appropriate corrective measures would be initiated prior to initiation of full-scale production.

(4) Normally, the IPR chairman will be a member of the materiel development agency, ARRADCOM in most cases. The IPR committee makes recommendations for decision by the designated approval authority (usually a Major

Subordinate Commander), with DARCOM/HQDA usually only in a reviewing role; however, for some high-visibility or complex items, DARCOM/HQDA may exercise IPR approval authority.

2–3. Initial requirements computation.

a. The Army Acquisition Objective (AAO) quantity for a new item of ammunition is determined by the ODCSRDA (DAMA–PPP in coordination with DAMA–CSM), based on rate studies conducted by CAA in accordance with AR 710–8 under the sponsorship of the ODCSOPS (DAMO–RQR). Rate study data may be modified through coordinated decisions by the DA Staff, day-to-day uncertainties related to fast-changing guidance, budget and materiel priorities, as well as other considerations.

b. The rate studies take into account the projected performance characteristics of the developmental item (range, accuracy, lethality), the US/Allies weapons densities projected for the study period (for gun/launcher fired munitions), the threat in terms of enemy formations, equipment and tactical doctrine, and the postulated warfighting scenario. The studies are computer-based simulations which estimate consumption for a specified period of combat. A more detailed description of this process is contained in chapter 4.

c. Developmental items which are slated to replace items in the inventory pose some special problems in this requirements determination process. Serviceable inventory rendered obsolete must be addressed. Disposal action, if required, is discussed in paragraph 2–9.

d. In the event existing inventory of an item scheduled to be phased out of the supply system is below the AAO, and the developmental item scheduled to replace it is not scheduled to be type classified for several years, another type of management decision must be made. If the existing inventory is low relative to the requirement, it may be considered prudent in terms of force readiness to buy new inventory knowing that it will be rendered obsolete when the replacement item is type classified. Alternatively, when it is estimated that the production base can respond quickly in the event of hostilities, the inventory of the older item may be deliberately allowed to decline to avoid significant stocks of obsolete items. Current alternatives to reduce or eliminate ammunition items from the stockpile include Foreign Military Sales (FMS), Grant Aid, Military Aid Prorams, regulated training attrition, testing and controlled demilitarization.

2–4. Procurement/Production.

a. The procurement/production phase follows development of requirements and apportionment of appropriated program funds through OSD, HQDA, and DARCOM to the operating agencies (ARRCOM, ARRADCOM, and MICOM) comptrollers. The National Inventory Control Point (NICP) at ARRCOM validates the continuing need for procurement of each item of ammunition and the comptroller certifies the funds and releases them to the procurement organization for acquisition.

b. Although ammunition requirements and budget programs are expressed as complete rounds, most items, except for small arms ammunition, are procured as components. The production organization breaks the rounds into procurable elements (typically, the projectile, fuze, cartridge case, propelling charge, explosive, primer). The procurement organization formulates contracts with government-owned contractor-operated (GOCO) plants and with private industry, while the production organization directs work at Government-owned Government-operated (GOGO) plants. In general, metal parts are procured from the private sector, and production of propellants and explosives and load, assembly, and pack (LAP) is accomplished at government facilities; however, propellant may be obtained from industry, or metal parts from GOCO plants. The selection, in cases where multiple sources (both within the Government and in private industry) are available to produce an item, is based on plant workloading and scheduling considerations, maintenance of the mobilization base, and economic considerations. An economic analysis of the sources is conducted to determine the low-cost mix, and the economic solution is evaluated against noneconomic factors, such as new item requirements, modernization, mobilization, skill retention, and personnel impact. The Army's industrial base for production of ammunition is discussed in detail in paragraph 3–4 which addresses the logistic support structure.

c. Once the production is assigned, the production manager monitors the production effort using production and delivery schedules and reports. Procurement contracts and production delivery schedules must consider not only direct Army-funded programs but also customer orders from various funding sources for the same ammunition items and components. Testing during this phase of the materiel life cycle will be production testing in accordance with AR 702–9. All production and delivery schedules must be integrated and keyed to the assembly of complete rounds at the LAP plant. Once completed, the round is shipped to its first destination, the designated CONUS depot or overseas port, using funding supplied by the operating agency comptroller from a separate budget line maintained for this purpose.

d. Procurement and production responsibility for most ammunition items is shared by ARRCOM and ARRADCOM. Generally, responsibility for management of an item in development belongs to ARRADCOM, while ARRCOM has responsibility for developed items approved for service use. Transition of the responsibility from ARRADCOM to ARRCOM occurs when design stability is achieved, the configuration baseline is established, the Technical Data Package (TDP) has been validated, and user feedback has documented user satisfaction. Detailed transition criteria and procedures are specified in DARCOM Regulation No. 70–1. The Release of Materiel for Issue Program is managed by DARCOM.

e. Standard items remain assigned to ARRCOM even when a Product Improvement Program (PIP) is ongoing or planned, and the PIP effort is executed by ARRADCOM. However, if the PIP effort should result in a new item or a model change, the item may transition back to ARRADCOM based on the established transition criteria.

f. ARRADCOM continues to provide engineering design support for items transitioned to ARRCOM as tasked by ARRCOM concerning engineering design relationships to assure life cycle integrity during initial production engineering.

2–5. Initial issue.

a. Preparation for initial troop issue and subsequent use throughout the materiel life cycle begins during the Conceptual Phase. During this Phase, initial consideration is given to the concepts of reliability, maintainability, compatibility, and standardization. Because of this, the ammunition development command (ARRADCOM) and the ammunition readiness command (ARRCOM) work jointly to prepare for the initial field of a developmental ammunition item.

b. HQDA establishes policies for the Army Integrated Logistic Support (ILS) Program and standards for logistical acceptability/supportability of materiel systems and end items. USALEA assesses the application/execution of ILS policy. DARCOM, as the principal materiel developer, has responsibility for actual implementation (planning/execution) of ILS policy in actions related to—

(1) Major Items

(2) Secondary Items

(3) Operations and maintenance, Army (OMA) Programs

(4) Supply Support

(5) Distribution

(6) Storage and Transportation

(7) Inventory Accounting

(8) Maintenance Support

(9) Maintenance Interservice Support Management

(10) Maintenance Engineering and Planning

(11) Preparation of Equipment Publications

(12) Depot Planning and Operations for Support of New or Modified Ammunition Materiel

(13) Quality Assurance

c. ARRCOM and ARRADCOM establish and maintain a single ILS point of contact and conduct other related activities as required by AR 700–127, and the DARCOM, ARRCOM, and ARRADCOM supplements. These activities enable implementation of ILS and are usually done in conjunction with the appropriate TRADOC centers, school, and test boards, USALEA, and other interested agencies. Essential to these actions is the formulation of several related plans and schedules. These are the—

(1) Materiel Fielding Plan (MFP) (AR 700–127)

(2) Basis of Issue Plan (BOIP) (AR 71–2)

(3) Coordinated Test Program (CTP) (AR 70–10)

(4) New Equipment Training Plan (NETP) (AR 350–35)

d. The prime objective of this activity is to field a new or improved equipment, enhance operational readiness, improve logistic support, and minimize the cost of system ownership. Coordinated effort is essential to develop MOS training programs and maintenance procedures, prepare and print operation and maintenance publications, and related materiel actions.

2–6. Storage.

a. General.

(1) Most munitions are produced long before their ultimate consumption; therefore, the storage of ammunition is an important logistics consideration. "Long-term storage" actually encompasses two phases of storage. First, there is the transportation and storage of the munitions until they are transported to the Army in the field. Second, there is the transportation and storage of the munitions by the Army in the field until consumed. For some items, the length of time they may remain in storage is measured in decades. This is an important consideration in the design of packing and packaging materials, storage plans and storage aids, as well as the design of ammunition storage facilities. In general, ammunition must be protected from moisture and should be protected from temperature extremes when feasible.

(2) Most of the Army's conventional ammunition is produced in Army Ammunition Plants (AAP's) and shipped from these plants to storage depots in CONUS and overseas (primarily Europe and Pacific areas). Exceptions are the three former Navy facilities (McAlester, Hawthorne, and Crane) transferred to the Army on 1 October 1977 as GOGOs. Hawthorne Army Ammunition Plant has since become a GOCO facility, effective 1 December 1980. End items of ammunition are stored in the plants to the maximum extent practical to avoid the expenditure of additional

transportation handling costs incurred at depots, especially in CONUS. A listing of the facilities in which ammunition is stored is contained in paragraph 3–5a.

b. *Use of open storage.* The DOD Explosive Safety Board (DDESB), by 18 December 1974 letter to the Military Services, announced the following standard for open/covered storage of ammunition:

(1) Open storage is a temporary expedient and should not be used in lieu of standard methods for long-term storage.

(2) Earth-covered magazine storage should be used wherever possible. In comparison with other methods, it provides a higher degree of protection and safety for the ammunition and surrounding targets, greater physical security, and reduced maintenance of the ammunition. The Board supports open revetted pad storage only under emergency or temporary conditions, not for permanent, long-term use. An example of an approved use for open storage is for bombs slated for demilitarization stored on revetted pads between magazines.

c. *Basic load storage facilities.* The Army has consistently sought to use earth-covered magazine storage in all long-term storage facilities. In those areas where selected vehicles are uploaded, the Army is preparing facilities to meet DDESB explosive safety standards and applicable standards for physical security.

2–7. Ammunition stockpile reliability.

a. The purpose of the Ammunition Stockpile Reliability Program (ASRP), per AR 702–6, is to provide a means of evaluating the operational readiness, serviceability, safety, reliability, and performance of ammunition in the stockpile and/or deployed for use in combat or training and to provide information necessary for decisionmaking in the overall logistic management of ammunition—retention, maintenance, modification, or replacement.

b. For each ammunition item or grouping of similar ammunition items of the ASRP, a representative sampling scheme is developed and samples are selected and subjected to controlled laboratory tests, functional tests, stockpile reliability test firings, and visual inspections to determine the reliability and condition of the current stockpile and identify trends which may affect the overall quality. Timely identification of undesirable trends allows the ammunition manager to minimize the cost of retention of unreliable and unsafe stocks, schedule required maintenance actions, or establish removal/replacement intervals or schedule for priority of issue and use.

2–8. Conventional ammunition maintenance.

a. Unlike other commodities, maintenance requirements for ammunition cannot be determined on the basis of predetermined yardsticks such as flying hours, miles driven, or hours of operation, The degree of conventional ammunition maintenance (see figure 2–2) will vary dependent upon deficiencies involved, and can range from normal preservation and packaging activities (i.e., derusting and repainting), usually performed at the retail/user level, to more hazardous operations of disassembly and reassembly with serviceable components, modification, and conversion, normally done at the wholesale level. The lesser degree of maintenance is normally required in order for the ammunition to have the capability to withstand long-term storage without degradation of the stockpile. The more extensive maintenance (renovation) is to correct deficiencies affecting safety and reliability of the ammunition which could cause malfunctions resulting in death or serious injury to the user, or extensive property damage and loss of expensive weapons and equipment.

b. Maintenance at the user level is normally limited to preservation and packaging, such as derusting, spot-painting, delinking, and relinking of small arms ammunition for functional training requirements, or limited repacking of small quantities. More extensive maintenance (renovation) is performed in theater at depots in the rear areas, and in depots in CONUS. In theater rear areas, depots are usually equipped to perform practically all levels of maintenance, thus precluding the need to retrograde items to CONUS solely for maintenance purposes.

c. In past years, conventional ammunition has been degrading to unserviceable status at a much greater rate than can be supported by annual maintenance programs. This situation was caused by funding constraints which impacted upon pay of personnel, design and development of Ammunition Peculiar Equipment (APE) (AR 700–20 and DARCOM Supplement thereto), and availability of components for renovation. Army plans are to allot sufficient resources to eliminate the maintenance backlog by the mid–1980's.

2–9. Disposal.

a. Disposal of ammunition is required to purge the distribution system of ammunition which became obsolete, excess, unserviceable, uneconomical to repair, and/or condemned/hazardous for continued storage, maintenance, and/or use. Disposal as addressed herein primarily pertains to ammunition disposal/demilitarization operations involving large quantities of ammunition. Demilitarization excludes the destruction of duds on firing ranges by Explosive Ordnance Disposal (EOD) personnel.

b. Methods of disposal may involve the following:

(1) Sales to foreign governments through an international logistics program for surplus, excess, and obsolete ammunition which is otherwise serviceable.

(2) Commercial contract demilitarization.

(3) Disassembly and retention of usable components and packaging materials, washout of explosive filler, and

reclamation of propellant and metal parts for reuse. Unserviceable, unsafe, and/or unreliable components are demilitarized to assure they are free of explosives or harmful chemicals, and mutilated to the extent they cannot be used for the originally intended purpose.

(4) Demilitarization by detonation or burning. While still a viable method for disposal, environmental considerations place an ever-increasing constraint on detonation and open burning.

c. Scrap metal is sold through property disposal offices.

d. Demilitarization is performed by personnel specifically trained in the procedures, methods, and hazards associated with destruction of ammunition.

e. Equipment used by the Army in demilitarization operations is provided through the Ammunition Peculiar Equipment (APE) program. The APE program is an Army organic program to design, develop, test, and fabricate APE for all depot operations involving ammunition. APE is provided to Army customers on free issue basis and to other services and international logistics customers on a reimbursable basis. Current funding for APE in support of the demilitarization program is in PAA (OMA prior to FY80). Commodity Centers for APE are the US Army Defense Ammunition Center and School, Savanna Army Depot Activity and the Ammunition Equipment Office, Tooele Army Depot. The APE Program is essential to the Army demilitarization program since such equipment is specialized and not otherwise available from commercial sources.

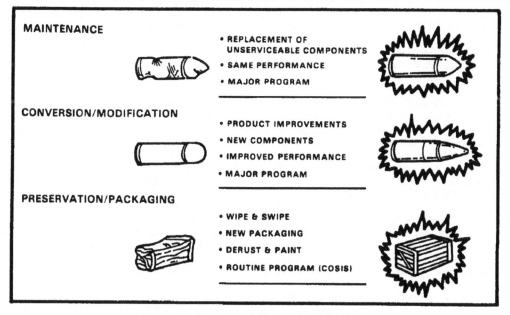

Figure 2-2. Conventional Ammunition Maintenance

Chapter 3
MANAGEMENT AND LOGISTIC SUPPORT STRUCTURE

3-1. The management structure—overview.

a. The HQDA management structure for ammunition parallels that for other commodities. Requirements determination and force structure accounting are the responsibility of the DCSOPS. Materiel acquisition program formulation and defense of the program in the budgetary process are the responsibility of the DCSRDA. Materiel distribution and maintenance requirements are the responsibility of the DCSLOG who likewise defends that portion of the Army budget.

b. The DCSOPS is the primary interface with TRADOC in the context of how the war will be fought and how our forces will be equipped and trained, with the intelligence community for opposing force capabilities and order of battle, and with Army major force commands for their assessment of our own tactics and force readiness. All provide major inputs, qualitative and quantitative, to the requirements determination process.

c. The DCSRDA is the primary interface with the materiel research, development, and acquisition community, DARCOM, and its subordinate materiel development and materiel readiness commands. Annually, DCSRDA provides DARCOM Army Acquisition Objectives (AAOs) based on programing rates furnished by DCSOPS. These AAOs, less asset projections, are the "first cut" of the procurement program, which is refined in detail, by priority and dollar ceiling, by the cognizant DARCOM major subordinate commands working with DCSRDA at a joint review—ARRADCOM for the development and initial acquisition program; ARRCOM for the balance of the procurement program. The missile community also is involved in this effort for rockets. MICOM is the NICP for VIPER and the XM77 grenades for the MLRS. While component parts are procured by MICOM, load, assemble, and pack is performed by ARRCOM. This refinement process is necessitated by considerations of most efficient use of dollars projected to be available in the budget versus the spread of the total AAO over the POM period. For instance, it may be necessary to procure one item one year and another item in the next year, due to an unacceptable cost penalty connected with stretching out production of each over a longer period. Likewise, in research and development, one program may be funded to the detriment of another when there are not sufficient funds projected to be available for a meaningful level of effort in both.

d. Upon final congressional approval of the annual budget request, the management of ammunition programs transfers to ARRCOM, ARRADCOM, and applicable PMS, in their respective spheres, with the apportionment of appropriated funds to those commands. Initial procurement of newly type-classified items is managed by ARRADCOM. The balance of ammunition procurement is managed by ARRCOM. ARRCOM also manages wholesale ammunition distribution (materiel management), surveillance, and maintenance activities in CONUS and maintains asset visibility and technical responsibility for surveillance and maintenance worldwide. CONUS wholesale ammunition is defined as that which is stored or moving between CONUS wholesale storage areas and has not been delivered to a "user" (TRADOC, FORSCOM installation, or CONUS port of embarkation).

e. With the exception of Crane Army Ammunition Activity (CAAA), Hawthorne Army Ammunition Plant (HWAAP), and McAlester Army Ammunition Plant (MCAAP), the CONUS depot operations are under the command of DESCOM. DESCOM ships ammunition as directed by ARRCOM and also performs surveillance and renovation under the technical direction of ARRCOM. The oversea depots and materiel management agencies are under command of the oversea commander and generally parallel the CONUS operations in their mission functions. These elements are part of the management structure and are the last link in their respective chains before the ammunition passes to the "user."

f. Movement of ammunition, both within CONUS and to oversea ports of discharge, is accomplished under procedures agreed to by the Military Departments and/or SMCA and is administered by MTMC. For a given fiscal year, ARRCOM and ARRADCOM budget for first destination transportation, and depots budget for second destination transportation to CONUS installations and CONUS ports of embarkation, as part of the OMA Appropriation. The military services budget for transportation and shipping, ocean terminal operations, and reimbursement of MTMC and MSC for expenses incurred. All modes/categories are reimbursable by the shipping command/service. CONUS outports and ocean shipping are industrially funded. Oversea ports are OMA funded. The oversea commands are responsible for movement from the ship's hook onward within the theater.

g. The bases for all transportation budget forecasts are annual oversea command call-forward projections (replenishments and prepositioned materiel buildups—all classes of supply) plus CONUS-originated "push" projections for all commodities. DARCOM aggregates these for the entire Army and furnishes them to ODCSLOG for review and validation. Port handling and ocean shipping forecasts are forwarded by ODCSLOG to MTMC and MSC, respectively.

h. Except for Korea, construction of new ammunition storage facilities and major modification or rehabilitation of existing facilities are the responsibility of the Corps of Engineers, in response to total Army-wide facilities requirements furnished by ODCSLOG. Major modifications are those exceeding the cost criteria for OMA funding. Land acquisition for new facilities overseas is the responsibility of the theater commander, as is acquisition through leasing of host nation ammunition facilities for US use. In USAREUR, ammunition storage facilities are programed through the host nation using NATO Infrastructure Funding. To date, however, this has supplied a relatively minor part of the total requirement. US participation in the NATO Infrastructure Program is normally limited to ensuring that user requirements are met. Design and construction are accomplished by the host nation. By agreement with the Republic of Korea, acquisition of ammunition storage facilities in Korea is that country's responsibility. The facilities are operated by Republic of Korea Army (ROKA) but jointly used by ROKA and EUSA under the Single Ammunition Logistics System—Korea (SALS–K). Separate asset identity is maintained and the US retains accountability arid control of both EUSA and WRSA earmarked for ROKA use in event of hostilities. US is also charged with quality assurance of these stocks while ROKA performs storage, maintenance, handling, and transportation functions under direction of EUSA in accordance with SALS–K MOA.

i. The Secretary of the Army is designated as the DOD Single Manager for Conventional Ammunition (SMCA) by DOD Directive 5160.65. The Commanding General (CG), DARCOM is delegated by the SMCA Charter the authorities of the Secretary of the Army for execution of SMCA operations with power to redelegate. The Executive Director for Conventional Ammunition (EDCA) is designated by CG, DARCOM, and the SMCA Charter for performance of the SMCA activities with power to carry out functions assigned to the CG, DARCOM.

j. ARRCOM is the principal field operating activity of the SMCA and is responsible for acquisition of Army fielded munitions items and assigned munitions of the other services. This includes production base support and procurement of items for all DOD services and other programs such as Security Assistance. Under the Single Manager concept, ARRCOM is also responsible for distribution, storage, maintenance, and disposal of Air Fore, Navy, Marine Corps, and Army stocks stored in CONUS wholesale installations. Requirements of all services are aggregated, and the services reimburse the Army for major maintenance and renovation work performed on their stocks. The Army, as the SMCA, budgets to support the care of supplies in storage (COSIS) workload,

k. ARRCOM coordinates with ARRADCOM to develop procurement and production strategy for new items and to ensure a smooth transition from the development phase to the operational or fielded phase of the materiel life cycle. ARRCOM/MPBMA ensures maintenance and modernization of the production base for currently fielded items, and in coordination with ARRADCOM, is responsible for development of an adequate production base for anticipated modernization items. The ARRCOM also coordinates with other major Army commands (MACOM) to develop materiel call forward plans, provide logistics and technical support, and other customer assistance as required.

l. The MPBMA is responsible for development, budgeting, and management of the major program to modernize the existing ammunition production base and expand it to provide for manufacture of newly developed items, at locations and against requirements specified by ARRCOM. MPBMA also manages the supporting manufacturing technology base through funding of projects to develop the most cost-effective manufacturing techniques and process controls.

3–2. The Management Structure—Headquarters, Department of the Army.

a. Office of the Deputy Chief of Staff for Research, Development, and Acquisition (ODCSRDA).

(1) *Director of Combat Support Systems (DAMA–CS).* Is the principal Army Staff Ammunition Management Executive (delegated by DCSRDA) with authority for integration and coordination of Army Staff efforts to increase the effectiveness of the Army's ammunition life cycle.

(2) *Munitions Division (DAMA–CSM), Combat Support Systems Directorate.* Serves as focal point on the Army Staff for overall management of Army conventional ammunition. This division handles all DA Staff actions pertaining to research, development, and acquisition of conventional munitions, production base modernization and expansion, and major management actions such as implementation of the SMCA efforts (a DOD mission), preparation and updating of the Army Ammunition Management System description, implementation of the CASPR recommendations, preparation and updating of the Army Ammunition Plan, and conduct of the DA Quarterly Ammunition Review (chaired by the Director, Combat Support Systems).

(3) *Research, Development, Test and Evaluation Programs and Budget Division (DAMA–PPR), Materiel Plans and Programs Directorate.* Responsible for issuance of fiscal guidance for Budget and POM to ODCSRDA commodity divisions and for assembly of division inputs into annual Army program for the RDTE Appropriation. Monitors release of program funds for execution.

(4) *Procurement Programs and Budget Division (DAMA–PPP), Materiel Plans and Programs Directorate.* Functions similar to (3), above, for the procurement appropriations, to include Procurement of Ammunition, Army. Also exercises supervision over requirements computations performed by the US Army Research, Development, and Acquisition Information Systems Agency (RDAISA).

(5) *Policy, Plans and Management Division (DAMA–PPM), Materiel Plans and Programs Directorate.* Responsible for planning, programing, and budgeting for maintenance of the inactive ammunition production base from the OMA appropriation and for industrial preparedness planning. Responsible for research, development, and acquisition policy, development test policy (AR 70–10), and production test policy (AR 702–9).

b. Office of the Deputy Chief of Staff for Operations and Plans (ODCSOPS).

(1) *Operations Readiness and Mobilization Directorate (DAMO–OD).* Assesses the adequacy of the Army Ammunition Management System to support operations and contingency planning, with emphasis on the current year. Provides current tactics, doctrine, and concepts and submits the data to DAMO–RQ for combat computer simulations. Maintains current MACOM Required Supply Rates (RSR) and basic load requirements. Provides current force structure and

current deployment sequence to DAMO–RQ for combat computer simulations. Provides and/or validates ammunition requirements for planning and assisting DCSRDA in program development in the following areas:

(a) Army Operational Projects.

(b) Army Non-Combat Requirements (Civil Disturbance).

(2) *Force Management Directorate (DAMO–FD).* Provides the DA Master Force File containing current and projected force structure and force deployment information to CAA which provides computational support to Total Army Analysis. Employs approved force structure in development of Logistics Structure and Composition System (LOGSACS) which supports POM development and is used by CAA for combat simulations and DARCOM for calculations of stockage objectives.

(3) *Combat Service Support Division (DAMO–RQL), Requirements Directorate.* Serves as the ODCSOPS single point of contact responsible for integration and coordination of all conventional ammunition actions within ODCSOPS. Establishes ammunition priorities and validates requirements for developmental ammunition to include LOA, ROC, and Letter Requirements (LR) contained in the Catalog of Approved Requirements Documents (CARDS). Develops current and projected weapons/munitions lists and provides this data for determining combat consumption rates. Obtains from TRADOC the POM and Extended Planning Annex doctrine and tactics to support combat computer simulations. Analyzes the simulations performed by CAA and recommends rates for use by ODCSLOG, ODCSRDA, and MACOMs in developing the Army Ammunition Plan. Provides ammunition consumption levels used in the conduct of the Total Army Analysis and OMNIBUS Studies. Provides and/or validates ammunition requirements for planning and assists ODCSRDA in program development for Post-D-Day consumption and ODCSLOG in determining stockage objectives.

(4) *Strategy, Plans and Policy Directorate (DAMO–SS).* Provides Extended Planning Annex and other force deployment sequences to DALO–RQ for combat computer simulations. Ensures that force structure and deployment data used in ammunition rate studies is coordinated with that provided to the Joint Planning System. Provides to DAMO–RQ allied forces data and assists in the development of weapons/munitions lists and rates to support those forces. Monitors the US ability to meet ammunition requirements of allies. Assesses political-military impact of rates and resulting stockage objectives. Provides and/or validates ammunition requirements for planning and assists DCSRDA in program development in the following areas:

(a) Special Contingency Stockpile (SCS) requirements.

(b) War Reserve Stocks for Allies (WRSA).

(c) Information on allies' ammunition status—

(1) Peacetime and wartime production capabilities; (2) Projected production by timeframe for ammunition; and (3) Current ammunition asset posture.

(5) *Training Support Division (DAMO–TRS), Training Directorate.* Exercises primary staff responsibility for the TAMS, establishing coordinated guidance for developing training ammunition requirements, maintains TAAC-validated requirements and transmits these to ODCSRDA for incorporation into the AMP, sets priorities within and between training ammunition procurement programs, prepares coordinated training ammunition authorizations for commands, and uses the Training Ammunition Management Information System (TAMIS) in managing Army ammunition assets expended in training. Provides and/or validates ammunition requirements for planning and assists DCSRDA in program development in the following areas:

(a) Training Ammunition authorizations for Active and Reserve Components,

(b) Training Ammunition requirements in support of mobilization.

(c) Training Ammunition authorizations in support of special operations, allied training, and other Federal activities.

c. Office of the Deputy Chief of Staff for Logistics (ODCSLOG).

(1) *Resources and Management Directorate (DALO–RM).* Serves as DA Program Director for OMA Program 7 (supply, maintenance, and transportation). Aggregates OMA Program 7 requirements within ODCSLOG and defends them in the Budget/POM process.

(2) *Ammo/Special Weapons Office (DALO–SMA), Supply and Maintenance Directorate.* Serves as the ODCSLOG single point of contact responsible for integration and coordination of all conventional ammunition actions within ODCSLOG. Determines war reserve stockage levels to support the force specified by ODCSOPS for the support period established by DOD and Army guidance. Computes distribution requirements, in coordination with ARRCOM and MACOMs, to meet specified stockage levels for war reserve, training, operations, special contingency projects, and security assistance requirements. Determine storage facility requirements, in coordination with MACOMs, and conveys new or upgraded facility requirements to Office, Chief of Engineers for programing, budgeting, and execution. Develops concepts, policies, plans, and procedural guidance for conventional ammunition allocation, distribution, stockpile reliability, maintenance, and disposal.

(3) *Plans, Readiness and Systems Directorate (DALO–PL).* Responsible for analysis of operations and contingency plans for logistic supportability and identification of logistic resource shortfalls. DA Staff responsibility to monitor development of overall logistics concepts, doctrine, and, in coordination with ODCSOPS, logistics force structure. Monitors force logistics readiness worldwide.

(4) *Transportation, Energy and Troop Support Directorate (DALO–TS).* Responsible for strategic mobility plans and

programs, and transportation force structure development. Principal concern for ammunition supply is intertheater life capability–port capacity and availability of ocean shipping. Acts as HQDA interface with MTMC and MSC.

d. Chief of Engineers (COE). Programing Division (DAEN–ZCP), Assistant Chief of Engineers (ACE). Serves as the COE single point of contact for integration and coordination of all conventional ammunition activities within COE, Responsible for planning, programing, and budgeting construction to support ammunition production and storage requirements except for those actions associated with PAA funding for construction of production facilities.

e. Other Army Staff agencies. Other Army Staff agencies retain responsibility for conventional ammunition program accomplishment within their assigned functional areas; e.g., ODCSPER (Physical Security, Explosive Safety, Civilian and Military Personnel), OCA (Army Budget, reprograming). Each staff agency will designate an organizational element as a single point of contact to coordinate ammunition management and SMCA matters within its agency.

3–3. Functional Interrelationships.

Organizational responsibilities described in the preceding portions of this section are portrayed schematically to each other and to specific tasks/events in the Budget/POM process in the following figures:

a. Figure 3–1—Procurement Program Formulation

b. Figure 3–2—Production Base Program Formulation

c. Figure 3–3—OMA Program (72) Ammunition Requirement & Funding System

d. Figure 3–4—RDTE Program Formulation.

PROCUREMENT PROGRAM FORMULATION (PAA, ACTIVITY 1)

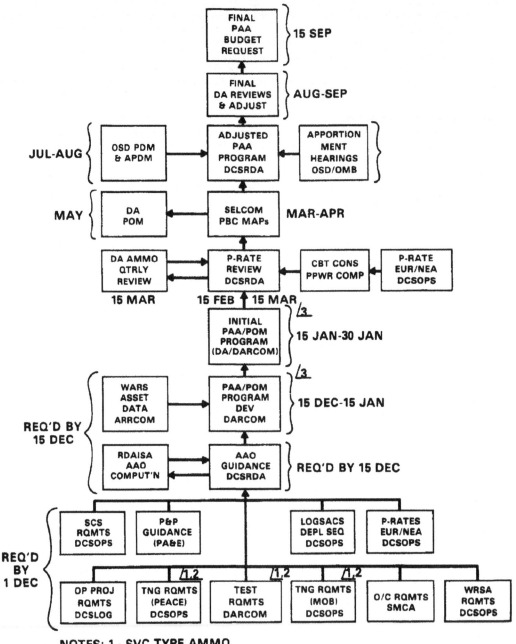

NOTES: 1 - SVC TYPE AMMO
2 - TNG PECULIAR AMMO
3 - CL V PORTION OF AMP

Figure 3-1. Procurement Program Formulation

PRODUCTION BASE PROGRAM FORMULATION (PAA, ACTIVITY 2)

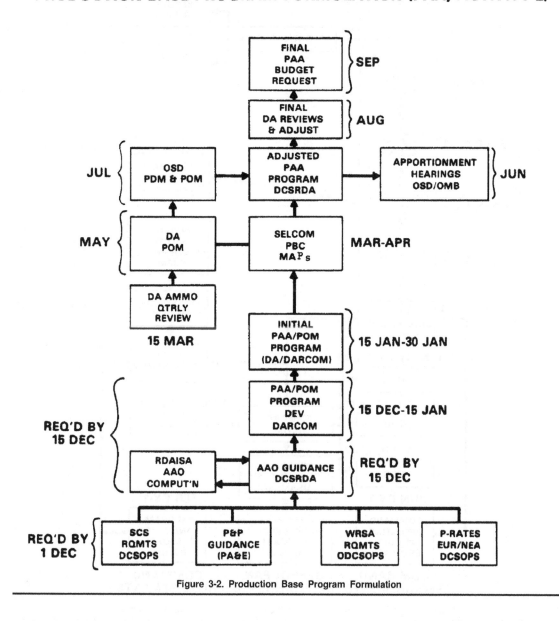

Figure 3-2. Production Base Program Formulation

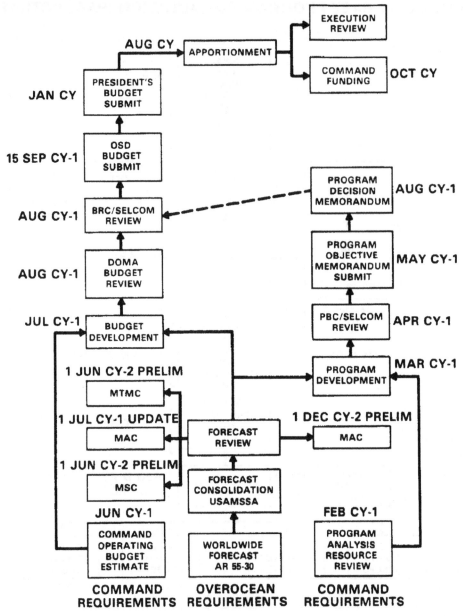

Figure 3-3. OMA Program (72) Ammunition Requirement & Funding System

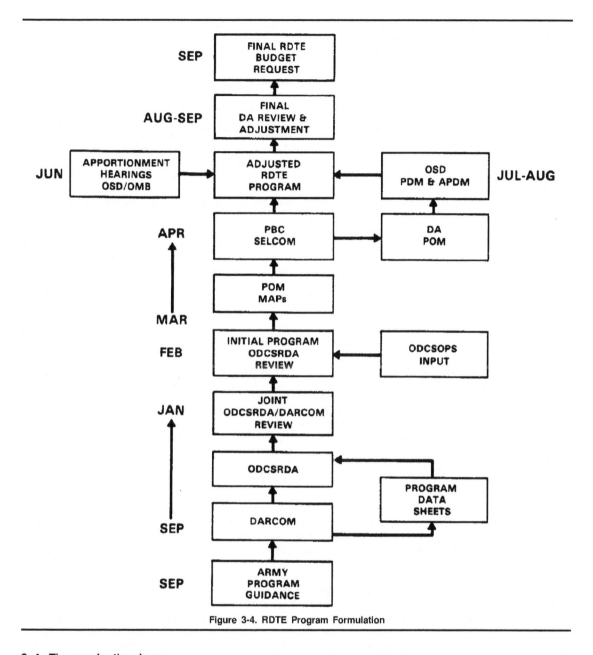

Figure 3-4. RDTE Program Formulation

3–4. The production base.

a. General. The ammunition production base is the national manufacturing complex required to produce metal parts and components, manufacture propellants and explosives, and to load, assemble, and pack ammunition components and end items. The production base consists of hundreds of current and planned producers categorized into three groups: GOGO facilities, GOCO facilities, and contractor-owned contractor-operated (COCO) facilities. There are 25 GOCO plants and 3 GOGO in existence and 1 GOCO being constructed. Twelve GOCO plants are in layaway status; the balance of the base is active. Also constituting part of the Government-operated segment of the production base are arsenal and laboratory facilities collocated with Army R&D activities. There are a total of 91 contractor-owned plants which utilize Government-owned plant equipment packages. The replacement value of the production base is in excess of $22 billion. The base comprises the hard core of our capability to equip and sustain the Army, as well as the Air Force, Navy, and Marine Corps, with ammunition during any armed conflict.

b. Description of base. Figure 3–5 depicts the location of all GOCO and GOGO production base facilities. Specific data concerning the current active and inactive Government-owned facilities and modernization plans is shown in appendix C. The private sector of the production base is of crucial importance to conventional munitions production. The most important source of metal parts for ammunition ranging from 20mm through 16-inch projectiles, cartridge cases, and fuzes is located in private industry which uses its own equipment as well as plant equipment provided by the Government. Figure 3–6 indicates the location of plant equipment packages throughout the United States. In addition, other plant equipment packages formerly assigned to producers (X-facility lines) are now in storage.

(1) For ammunition alone, the Army has approximately 472 Production Schedule Planning Agreements (DD Form 1519) with private industry to provide for rapid conversion of facilities from peacetime to wartime production requirements upon mobilization. There are also 542 Production Schedules for Mobilization Planning Purposes in the GOCO/GOGO sector for a combined total of 1014 Production Schedules. These Government planning agreements with industry allow for contractor facilitization prior to mobilization, primarily using Government-owned equipment, and form an integral portion of the Army's mobilization base.

(2) The GOGO/GOCO plants provide the bulk of propellant and explosive manufacturing capability as well as the larger portion of load, assembly, and pack capability while private industry provides nearly all the Government's needs for metal parts, fuzes, components, and packaging. In general, these metal parts are supplied to the GOCO plants where they are loaded, assembled, and packed into complete rounds for distribution to the military users.

c. Production base management and planning.

(1) *Single manager—* The Secretary of the Army has been designated responsibility as DOD Single Manager for Conventional Ammunition (SMCA). The SMCA is assigned a wide range of conventional ammunition items of the Army, Navy, Air Force, and Marine Corps, and is responsible for procurement, production, related production base facilities, and wholesale supply, maintenance, renovation, demilitarization and disposal and transportation of these items.

(a) The Executive Director for Conventional Ammunition (EDCA) is assigned the mission to manage and execute the DOD SMCA program. The EDCA, under the authority of the CG DARCOM, manages and executes the SMCA program in accordance with the authority and responsibilities prescribed in DOD Directive 5160.65 and the SMCA charter. The EDCA is the SMCA focal point in the National Capital Region and interfaces with all levels of the DOD organization involved in the execution of the SMCA mission.

(b) The Commanding General, ARRCOM, has been delegated responsibility for the conduct of field operations for the SMCA.

(2) *SMCA support—* In support of the SMCA, the US Army has dedicated ammunition production base planning and management activities at DA staff level and within DARCOM and two of its principal subordinate commands, ARRCOM and ARRADCOM.

(a) The MPBMA under ARRCOM performs planning, programing, and management functions for ammunition production base modernization and expansion efforts of the DOD. Design and construction of these modernization and expansion projects is the responsibility of the Chief of Engineers. The US Army Engineer Division, Huntsville, is responsible for technical and fiscal management of construction activities.

(b) ARRADCOM is the technological base for production base operation, modernization, and expansion through development of new MMT, design of initial production of facilities (IPF), mass production process equipment planning, and conduct of initial procurement. ARRADCOM also initiates new item base transitioning to ARRCOM and technical support to ARRCOM for transitioned base facilities and equipment.

(c) ARRCOM manages the transitioned production base through implementation of the Army's Industrial Preparedness Program (AR 700–90) and is responsible for complete procurement/production after initial production. ARRCOM also manages the annual Production Support and Equipment Replacement (PS&ER) program for active GOCO plants. The PS&ER program is to sustain the ability to meet current and planned production requirements through maintaining the design capacity of equipment and facilities by equipment replacement and correction of normal deterioration through repair.

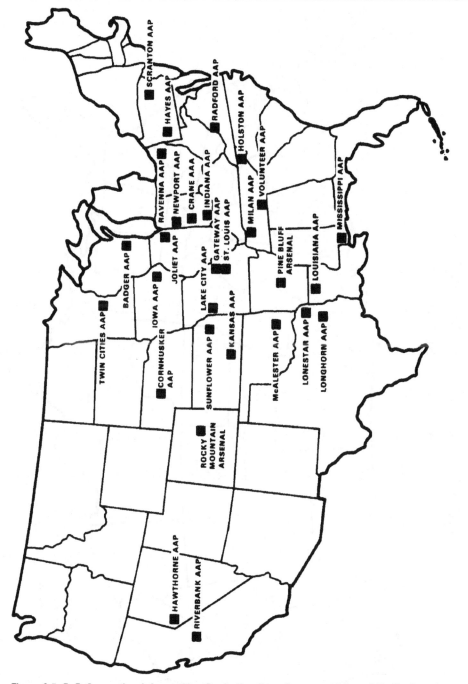

Figure 3-5. DoD Conventional Ammunition Production Base Government Owned Facility Locations

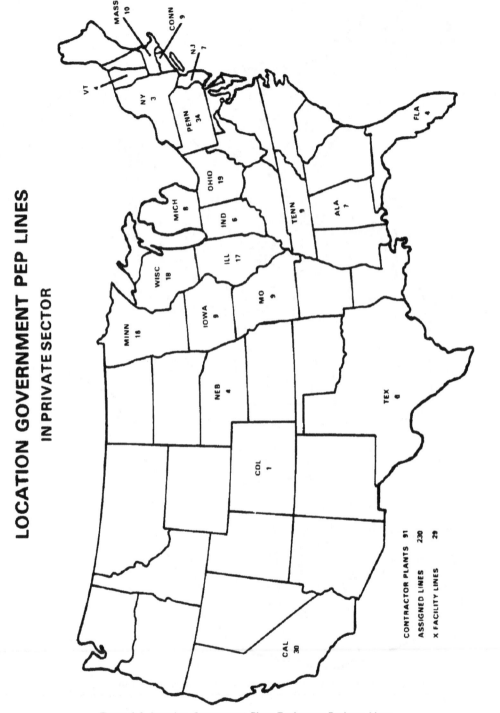

Figure 3-6. Location Government Plant Equipment Package Lines

(3) *Plans and Management Systems—* There is a well-executed planning system, the Production Base Plan (PBP)/ Production Base Analysis, which records the comparatively recent munitions production base experience and is the basis of information for necessary justification and direction for structuring the retention, layaway, and maintenance of the current base. A DOD Munitions Production Base Modernization and Expansion (M&E) plan is also maintained and periodically updated which controls the total M&E effort at the project level at all Government and commercial facilities. Other relevant management information systems include Plant Equipment Package Management Information System (PEPMIS) and the Production Base Maintenance and Layaway Data Base. These plans and management systems effectively implement the Army's Industrial Preparedness Program (IPP) guidelines and policy as required in AR 700–90.

d. Long-term problems of the base.

(1) Base age and resource availability. The current ammunition production base is, to a large degree, of World War II and Korean War vintages, with many facilities which are obsolete and difficult to maintain. Since the establishment of the base, there have been rapid technological advances as well as acutely increased attention to environmental and occupational safety and health factors. These influences have resulted in entirely new and diverse families of ammunition, major improvements to existing ammunition components, new and increasingly more complex manufacturing/ production processes, and the recognition of the fact that ammunition plants present serious safety and environmental health issues requiring systematic elimination. Compounding these has been the decreased availability of skilled ammunition base personnel due to normal attrition and budgetary restrictions, plus higher skill requirements to operate the more efficient but more sophisticated modern plant equipment.

(2) *Commitment to base during peacetime.* Another issue associated with the production base has been the some- times changing US commitment to base maintenance as a vital factor in our nation's defense. The base historically has contracted severely in peacetime, often with the virtual writeoff of billions invested in the crisis of war, only to be continually revived with still larger investments at the outset of each new emergency. This situation has a significant impact not only on the size and quality of the physical base but also seriously affects the private corporations involved in its support. A declining peacetime procurement environment is generally followed by a declining interest in commercial producer participation in mobilization planning since producers are not remunerated for this planning. Additionally, many capable former producers have declined to participate in ammunition production, not wanting to be labeled "merchants of death" and because of the difficulties of compliance with nonemergency Government procure- ment regulations and adverse treatment which they have received from Government regulatory and legislative bodies.

(3) *Changing ammunition requirements.*

(a) Another part of the production base issue in peacetime is fluctuating requirements and the effect on requirements of revised/updated threat (size, sustainability, weapons/munitions, warning time, and buildup rate), OSD guidance (duration of conflict, allies assumptions, production bases constraints) and Army plans (force structure, deployment sequence, POMCUS size, and weapons/munitions). This creates a continuously changing environment causing widely fluctuating requirements for ammunition production. Uncertainty as to availability of new developmental weapons and their relative lethality further complicates the requirements picture as well as the problem of balancing standard ammunition stocks and lead-time-constrained base resources.

(b) Some scenarios also plan for relatively short periods of war where a slowly reacting base, or portions of it, might not seem needed. However, others point to the distasteful choices available in the absence of a sustaining base if short wars become protracted. Lack of attention to the needs of the base results in extending the leadtime necessary for start-up and acceleration of production in emergencies. As the temperature of the base drops from warm to cold, its ability to expand rapidly is seriously impaired.

e. Program for base modernization and expansion. Detailed FYDP coverage of this program is contained in the Production Base Plan, annex C of the Army Ammunition Plan.

f. Laidaway production base operations and maintenance.

(1) *General.* ARRCOM is responsible for management of production base operations and maintenance. As some 87 percent of base facilities are over 20 years old, the capability of plants to respond in mobilization situations is a great concern. Nowhere is this concern more apparent than in laidaway base workloading and maintenance. As opposed to "warm" portions of the production base, standby or laidaway elements often do not have sufficient personnel or funding resources to maintain essential portions of their facilities.

(2) *Impact.* Due to the shortfall in funding resources, laidaway elements of the base have received only minimum levels of maintenance. The effect of reduced maintenance is to reduce the reactivation responsiveness of the production base. Experience with start-up of selected laidaway base elements proves that base readiness is seriously compromised due to the increased time and money required to repair urgently needed facilities. Although maintenance of the base is costly, some of the alternatives appear costlier; e.g., an increase in ammunition stocks, and related support needs, to equalize the diminished base readiness, or acceptance of appreciable loss in total readiness.

(3) *Industrial comparisons.* Since 1974 the size and value of the laidaway base have more than doubled due to

deactivations and inflation. Costs of basic standby elements, such as utilities and personnel, have also risen dramatically. The overall dollar resources committed to the base, however, have remained static. An analysis by ARRCOM indicates that the maintenance resource commitment to the inactive base should be on the order of 1 percent of the base replacement value; however, funding has averaged until recently approximately .05 percent of the replacement value.

3–5. Storage system.

a. Following is a list of all Army DESCOM depots which store conventional, as well as other munitions, for the Army, Air Force, Navy, and Marine Corps in CONUS as of 31 December 1981. This list excludes upload areas, training areas, and other small storage areas. The net square feet data were extracted from the JCAP Storage Manager's Handbook and the DA Storage Space Management Report. Capacity data are based on optimal storage conditions.

Table 3–1
Army DESCOM Depots Storage Capacities—CONUS

Location	Net Square Feet (thousands)	Storage Capacity (short tons)
Anniston Army Depot	3,995	570,714
(Anniston Army Depot)	(2,272)	(324,571)
(Lexington Blue Grass Army Depot Activity)	(1,723)	(246,143)
Letterkenny Army Depot	3,744	534,857
(Letterkenny Army Depot)	(1,679)	(239,857)
(Savanna Depot Activity)	(2,065)	(295,000)
Tooele Army Depot	9,110	1,301,429
(Tooele Army Depot)	(2,227)	(318,143)
(Pueblo Depot Activity)	(1,975)	(282,143)
(Fort Wingate Depot Activity)	(1,096)	(156,571)
(Navajo Depot Activity)	(1,634)	(233,429)
(Umatilla Depot Activity)	(2,178)	(311,143)
Red River Army Depot	1,354	193,429
Seneca Army Depot	1,439	205,571
Sierra Army Depot	2,745	392,143
CONUS TOTAL	22,387	3,198,143

b. These CONUS depots are operated by DESCOM located at Chambersburg, Pennsylvania, a subordinate command of DARCOM. ARRCOM also operates three formal naval installations with about 1.8 million short tons capacity, as well as plants and arsenals with a total of slightly under 0.5 million short tons capacity. Collectively, this represents about 5.5 million short ton capacity in the CONUS Wholesale System. Figure 3–7 displays CONUS ammunition storage locations geographically. An assessment of the capability of the CONUS depots to effect resupply to an active theater of operations at currently envisioned rates resulted in identification of deficiencies in materiel handling and communications/ADP capabilities. Resources to correct these deficiencies are the subject of continuing review in the planning, programing, and budgeting cycle.

c. Each major OCONUS commander has various ammunition storage facilities under his direct responsibility/command—

(1) *Pacific Area.* As of 31 December 1981, the Pacific Area had about 605,000 short tons of storage capacity, which was concentrated primarily in Japan and Korea as follows:

Table 3–2
Army DESCOM Depots Storage Capacities—OCONUS (Pacific)

Location	Net Square Feet (thousands)	Storage Capacity (Short tons)
Japan:		
Akizuki Army Depot	304	46,429
(Akizuki Army Depot)	(169)	(24,143)
(Kawakami Depot Activity)	(100)	(14,286)
(Hiro Depot Activity)	(56)	(8,000)
Korea:		
SALS–K Installations (29)	3913	558,955
PACIFIC TOTAL		605,384

(2) *European Area.* As of 31 December 1981, USAREUR had 838,000 short tons of storage capacity on the continent and in the United Kingdom. The largest of the sites was as follows:

Table 3–3
Army DESCOM Depots Storage Capacities—OCONUS (Europe)

Location	Net Square Feet (thousands)	Storage Capacity (short tons)
United Kingdom		
Bramely	689	98,429
Caerwent	573	81,857
Italy		
Camp Darby	334	47,714
Benelux		
Sugny	66	9,429
Barronville	110	15,714
Germany		
Miesau/Weilerbach	1,860	265,714
Saarland Sites (4)	98	14,000
Fischbach	196	28,000
Bruchsal	168	24,000
Dahn	131	18,714
Kriegsfeld	150	21,429
Muenster	110	15,714
Bamberg	102	14,572
Koeppern	270	38,571
Viernheim	155	22,143
Other	854	122,000
EUROPE TOTAL	5,866	838,000

Notes:
The other capacity (122,000 short tons), listed above, is spread among 30–plus sites whose individual capacities range from medium to very small.

d. Each major command (CONUS and OCONUS) requisitions ammunition directly from the National Inventory Control Points (ARRCOM for conventional munitions and MICOM for missiles). CAMO-PAC performs this function collectively for the Pacific. These requisitions are analyzed by the NICP to determine the location for most cost-effective shipping, considering age, type, condition, lot size, and quantity.

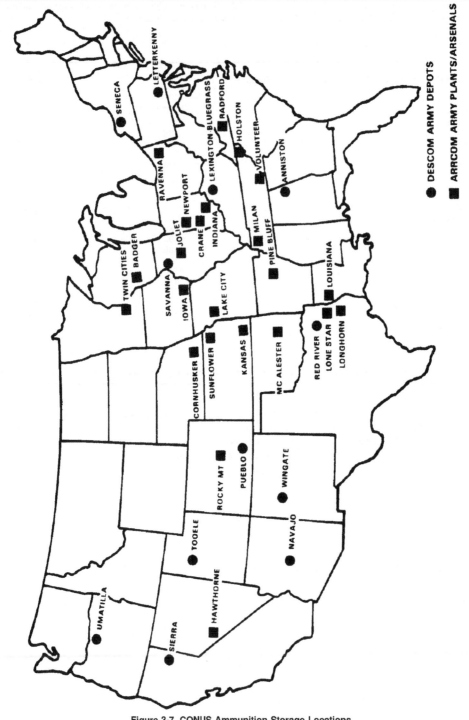

Figure 3-7. CONUS Ammunition Storage Locations

3–6. Transportation system.

a. The transportation system that provides for the movement of Army ammunition is essentially the same in peace or war. The principal difference between current resupply operations and an emergency or mobilization situation is in the quantities of ammunition moved.

b. Specific export shipment procedures are displayed in figure 3–8 and include the following:

(1) ARRCOM (NICP) receives the requisitions and determines asset availability and special consideration such as the necessity for shipping from specific sites or to meet specific ammunition characteristics. Based on that data, source/terminal cost analyses are made to determine which shipping source will provide lowest overall landed cost consistent with customers' requirements. Also, during this process, the requirements are assembled into shipload segments. It should be noted that during mobilization, the theater priority, depot assets and capabilities, carrier equipment, ship berthing dates, and terminals will also impact on selection of the supply sources.

(2) Having accomplished these tasks, ARRCOM requests (through the appropriate MTMC area command) MSC to berth a ship at the cost effective terminal on a date consistent with customer requirements, supply source, and carrier capabilities.

(3) Once a confirmed ship on berth date is received, ARRCOM prepares a ship planning message through semiautomated means. This message, dispatched to the several activities indicated in figure 3–8, provides a complete listing of the ammunition planned for that ship, an estimated overseas arrival date, and the destination terminal. The data in the message is retained on file in the SMCA computer as the data base for an intransit visibility file.

(4) The planning message also serves as a cargo offering to MTMC for routing purposes, and MTMC automatically releases the requisitioned items for movement from the supply source to the loading terminal. This precludes the shippers from having to request release of each shipment unit. As the material is shipped, the shippers transmit reports of shipment (REPSHIP) to all concerned parties. Terminals and overseas consignees use the information to plan their operations and storage requirements.

(5) After the loaded ship sails, an advance report of shipment is sent to all customers providing any known changes in tonnages planned versus loaded. When the manifest for that ship is received by ARRCOM, it is reconciled with the planned load, the intransit visibility file is updated, and a final report of shipment is dispatched. Subsequently, when the ship arrives at its first overseas port of call, the intransit file is updated to show that the ammunition is in transit in the theater.

(6) The system provides intransit visibility from the time of requisition until the ammunition is received in the overseas theater. This visibility provides the customer with a continuing status of ammunition items that are received in the theater. It also provides the overseas commander the flexibility to divert intransit ammunition consistent with combat needs or other requirements. Likewise, it facilitates planning for direct movement to theater locations bypassing storage depots, provides constant intelligence on inbound ammunition shipments, and provides firm planning data to allow scheduling of intertheater transportation.

(7) The procedure described above, which is largely a manual one, has been in use for over 12 years. Modeling and other computer-assisted techniques are being developed and analyzed for adoption by ARRCOM with the objective of enhancing system responsiveness.

c. Ammunition is normally moved by surface modes of transportation. Because of the substantial amounts of ammunition required to support large force deployments, intertheater movement of ammunition resupply by airlift will be on an exception basis. Intertheater airlift is the responsibility of the Military Airlift Command (MAC) (US Air Force).

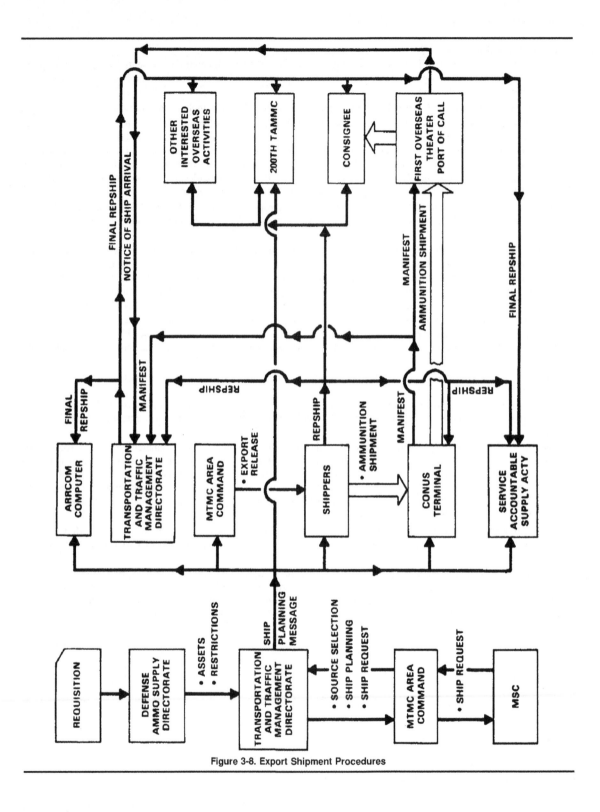

Figure 3-8. Export Shipment Procedures

d. The extensive US commercial surface transportation industry moves Army ammunition from its origin at a production plant or depot to the air or sea port of embarkation. The US rail system transports the majority of the Army ammunition tonnages, supplemented by the commercial trucking industry. The inherent capability of rail transportation to sustain the movement of large tonnages enables this mode to be highly effective and efficient. The responsiveness and flexibility of truck transport makes this mode more suitable for the movement of small lot shipments to seaports and high-priority shipments to air ports of embarkation. The current capacity of the US commercial surface transportation system is adequate to meet known emergency or mobilization military transportation needs.

e. While the physical capacity of the transportation system is adequate, experience indicates that the rail system needs rehabilitation. To correct this weakness in the system, the Army has developed a Railroads for National Defense Program, which identifies a network of strategic rail corridors and is intended to improve rail lines in those corridors. Analyses of the outloading capabilities of ammunition shipping installations are made periodically, and facilities, which are determined to be required, are then included in the DARCOM modernization plan.

f. The connecting link between the Army shipper (ammunition depot or plant) and the commercial transportation industry is provided by MTMC. MTMC serves as DOD's traffic manager in CONUS as well as common-user ocean terminal service operator in CONUS and certain overseas ports.

g. Ammunition is outloaded for oversea shipment at US ammunition ports. The current ammunition outloading capability at these ports is expressed below in terms of sustained ship outloading capability.

Table 3–4
Sustained Ship Outloading Capability

	Breakbulk	Container	Total
Military Ocean Terminal (MTMC), Kings Bay, GA (Transferred to USN 1 Jul 78)	1	—	1
Military Ocean Terminal (MTMC), Sunny Point, NC	4 or	1	4
Naval Weapons Station (USN), Earle, NJ	3		3
Naval Weapons Station (USN), Concord, CA	2		2
		Total	10

h. The Army recognizes that the current CONUS ammunition port outloading capability is insufficient to meet known requirements. Construction is underway to upgrade Military Ocean Terminal, Sunny Point, to a sustained loading capability of six ships— two containers and four breakbulk vessel support systems. For these improvements, projects costing $32.0 million were approved by Congress in 1979 (FY80). The Navy has agreed to upgrade the capability of NWS Earle to sustain the outloading of six ships. Resources have been programed by the Navy for this purpose. The Army transferred the ammunition facilities at Kings Bay to the Navy effective 1 July 1978 for use as a submarine base.

i. The MSC (US Navy) is responsible for providing sealift support to the services during both peace and war. MSC is also responsible for the development of plans and techniques which would enable the expansion of sealift capabilities during emergencies or mobilization. The US capability to rapidly expand sealift assets during emergencies comes from three principal sources:

(1) the MSC nucleus dry cargo fleet (27 government-owned or chartered ships), which is DOD's organic common-user sealift capability;

(2) the National Defense Reserve Fleet (NDRF) (149 ships), administered by the Maritime Administration, is a standby capability of largely older commercial merchant ships maintained in various states of readiness to support national emergencies or contingencies; and finally,

(3) the US Merchant Marine provides the bulk (288 ships) of the ready sealift capability to support military operations. During emergencies short of mobilization, US flag ship owners are committed to provide sealift resources (125 ships) to MSC under the Sealift Readiness Program. Upon mobilization, the US flag fleet can be requisitioned for defense purposes. Additionally, during a NATO emergency, it is planned that part of the sealift support to reinforce NATO will be provided by NATO-member merchant fleets.

j. Upon arrival in the oversea theater, Army ammunition is offloaded from ships at either military or commercial (host nation) ports and moved to destination by military or civilian contract truck assets and/or host nation(s) rail system. Host nation inland waterway transportation can also be used when advantageous. Control of host nation commercial transportation assets is exercised by that nation, and during wartime the allocation of resources to US forces is normally determined by US-host nation agreements. US unified commanders are responsible for the control, allocation, and management of US military transportation assets and for coordinating use of host nation civilian transportation assets. In Korea, munitions offloading and transporting to inland destinations is an ROKA responsibility and is performed under the SALS–K Memorandum of Agreement.

k. The procedures and techniques used to provide transportation service during peacetime are intentionally similar to those needed to meet the vastly expanded demands of an emergency or mobilization. Army requirements, together with those of the other Services, are examined from a transportation standpoint in the joint planning process. Various analytical techniques are used to test transport capabilities, identify system shortfalls, and recommend improvements. The three military transportation operating agencies (MTMC, MAC, and MSC) and the oversea commanders maintain liaison and coordination with the commercial carriers and Governmental agencies involved in providing the Army its transportation support. Through these efforts, the Army is able to keep abreast of system changes, to evaluate their impact on Army requirements, and to take action when necessary.

l. A major challenge facing the Army is to determine the proper level of containerization for the Army ammunition distribution system. Containerization affects the entire ammunition distribution system from production plant to firing battery with transportation being only one aspect of the system. A total systems approach has been initiated to achieve a throughput capability for containerized. conventional munitions of 1,000 containers per day. Ammunition plant and depot modernization programs are being developed by DARCOM to support this requirement and to correspond with the port modernization program.

Chapter 4
DETERMINATION OF CONVENTIONAL AMMUNITION RATES AND REQUIREMENTS

4–1. Ammunition rates determination process.

a. Reference. AR 710–8, dated 3 January 1975.

b. General. Scenarios, rates, force structure, and unit deployments are the driving factors for determination of ammunition acquisition and distribution objectives. Types of rates currently in use and the evolution of rate determinations are described in the following sections.

c. Definitions.

(1) *Ammunition rate.* A quantity expressed in rounds or units, per weapon, per day. For bulk allotment items, it is expressed in other units of measure, such as each or pounds per 1,000 men per day.

(2) *Programing rate (P–Rate).* A theater combat rate developed to assist the ARSTAF in determining the ammunition requirements for the last year of the POM.

(3) *Distribution rate (D–Rate).* A theater combat rate developed to assist the ARSTAF and MACOM commanders in determining the type and quantity of ammunition which will be made available to the designated MACOM. This asset constrained distribution requirement is normally developed and issued for the near term as a basis for actual distribution actions.

(4) *Requirement rate (R–Rate).* A theater combat rate developed to assist the ARSTAF in determining the ammunition requirements for the near term; actually a near-term P–Rate.

Note. The concept of an R–Rate study will be of utility in the asset distribution decision process.

d. Policy.

(1) One or more sets of theater combat rates will be developed, as required, for use in planning the distribution of current assets (distribution rates/D–Rates) and for use in procurement and production base support planning and programing (program rates/P–Rates).

(2) Theater combat rates (P– and D–Rates) will be reviewed at least annually, and revised as often as required to reflect—

(a) New concepts of organization and/or operations.

(b) Introduction of improved weapons and ammunition (modernization).

e. Concept. Theater combat rates will be used for the following purposes:

(1) *Distribution Rates (D–Rates).*

(a) As a basis for determining theater war reserve levels authorized by AR 11–11 and for validating MACOM requisitions.

(b) As a guide for computing resupply of active oversea commands.

(c) As a guide for establishing initial stockage and resupply in a newly activated theater.

(2) *Programing rates (P–Rates).* As a basis for computing the ammunition AAO.

(3) *Requirement Rates (R–Rate).*

(a) As a basis for computing the line-by-line PWRMS requirement which will be reviewed by HQDA for item availability.

(b) As the basis for theater storage objectives, storage facilities construction programs, call forward programs, and both follow-on requisitioning and distribution transactions.

(c) A consistent statement of the true requirement for a given theater.

f. Responsibilities.

(1) The DCSOPS (DAMO–RQ) has primary DA Staff responsibility for the development of theater combat ammunition rates.

(2) The DCSLOG (DALO–SM) has DA Staff responsibility for publishing SB 38–26, which contains the DA-approved D–Rates for the theaters for a specified timeframe, and for computing ammunition distribution requirements based on the approved D–Rates or R–Rates.

(3) The DCSRDA (DAMA–PPP in coordination with DAMA–CSM) has DA Staff responsibility for computing the ammunition AAOs based on approved P–Rates

g. Approval. Recommended P–Rates, D–Rates, and R–Rates are developed by ODCSOPS in coordination with the DA Staff and approved by the ODCSOPS chaired Study Advisory Group (SAG).

4–2. Ammunition programing requirements.

a. Reference. AR 710–8, dated 3 January 1975.

b. Ammunition Programing (P–Rate) Study. An ammunition programing (P–Rate) study will be conducted on an as-required basis dependent on the results of the ODCSOPS (coordinated with DA Staff) annual review of the current study and its application to the last year of the upcoming POM period. Study data in the annual review will include—

(1) US Forces/Units (size/composition).

(2) US deployment sequence.

(3) US weapon/munition lists.

(4) US tactics and doctrine.

(5) Scenario, threat, and deployment sequence.

(6) Study assumptions (example: warning/mobilization time).

(7) OSD guidance for upcoming POM period.

c. Annual review. The annual review could result in selected weapon system rates being changed as opposed to conducting a new ammunition programing study. Selected rate changes would be coordinated with the DA Staff and approved by DCSOPS.

d. Decision. When a decision is made to conduct an ammunition programing study, the following sequence of events will occur—

(1) DA Staff and MACOM notified of upcoming study effort.

(2) Study Advisory Group (SAG) formed by ODCSOPS (DAMO–RQ). Members of the SAG will include representatives from OASA(RDA), ODCSLOG, ODCSRDA, OACSI, OCSA(PA&E), DARCOM, TRADOC, CAA, and the appropriate theater.

(3) SAG develops and approves the study tasker, to include the objectives, scope, and assumptions, and then forwards the tasker to CAA for conduct of the study (DAMO–RQ).

(4) SAG meetings are conducted on an as-required basis with the primary emphasis on advising and providing assistance to CAA in the study effort.

(5) Major input data for the programing study reflects the force structure, equipment, and ammunition scheduled to be employed by the force in the last year of the POM. Since the focus of the study is on the last year of the POM, equipment, both modern and existing, is played to the extent that it will be fielded. Ammunition played will include both modern and selected existing munitions.

(6) SAG will make rate changes as required to compensate for new developments which would normally have changed one or more of the major study assumptions. Justification for each rate change will be fully documented.

(7) Proposed P–Rates are staffed and presented to ODCSOPS for DA Staff approval.

e. Computation of ammunition programing requirements.

(1) DA-approved P–Rates are provided by ODCSOPS(DAMO–RQ) to ODCSRDA(DAMA–PP).

(2) ODCSRDA (DAMA–PPP in coordination with DAMA–CSM) will determine the ammunition AAO based on the ODCSOPS (DAMO–FD) LOGSACS file/computer tape for the last year of the POM period. The LOGSACS file is reviewed/validated semiannually by the DA Staff. The validation process is conducted prior to the publication of the winter and summer LOGSACS file, with the file being available to the "users" about 1 July and 1 December. In addition to force size and composition this file will contain the deployment sequence based on a scenario directed by OSD. (See app B for detailed discussion of LOGSACS.)

4–3. Ammunition distribution requirements.

a. Reference. AR 710–8. dated 3 January 1975.

b. Ammunition distribution (D–Rate) study. An ammunition distribution (D–Rate) study will be conducted on an as-required basis dependent on the results of the ODCSOPS (coordinated with DA Staff) annual review of the current studies. Study data in the annual review will include—

(1) US Forces/Units (size/composition).

(2) US deployment sequence.

(3) US weapon/munitions lists.

(4) US tactics and doctrine.

(5) Scenario, threat, and deployment sequence.

(6) Study assumptions (example: warning/mobilization time).

(7) OSD and Army guidance or applicable allied force structures and tactical doctrine.

c. Annual review. The annual review could result in selected weapon system rates being changed as opposed to conducting a new ammunition distribution study. Selected rate changes would be coordinated with the DA Staff and appropriate theater commander and approved by ODCSOPS.

d. Decision. When a decision is made to conduct an ammunition distribution study, the following sequence of events will occur—

(1) DA Staff and MACOM notified of upcoming study effort.

(2) SAG formed by ODCSOPS (DAMO–RQ). Members of the SAG will include representatives from OASA(-RDA), ODCSLOG, ODCSRDA, OACSI, OCSA(PA&E), DARCOM, CAA, and the appropriate theater.

(3) SAG develops and approves the study tasker, to include the objectives, scope, and assumptions, and then forwards the tasker to CAA for conduct of the study (DAMO–RQ).

(4) Major input data for the distribution study reflects the force structure, equipment, and ammunition scheduled to be employed by the force during the year of the study. ODCSOPS (DAMO–RQL) will, in connection with the ammunition program analyst (DAMA–CSM), validate the ammunition to be played and specify which munitions will be "capped" at specific quantities.

(5) SAG meetings are conducted on an as-required basis with the primary emphasis on advising and providing assistance to CAA in the study effort.

(6) CAA submits the ammunition distribution rates to the SAG for review. On completion of SAG review, proposed distribution rates are forwarded to appropriate theater commander for comment.

(7) The DA staff and SAG analyzes the theater's input, with supporting rationale, and applies rate changes where appropriate.

(8) CAA provides proposed distribution rates to ODCSOPS (DAMO–RQ) for DA Staff approval.

e. Computation of ammunition distribution requirements.

(1) ODCSOPS (DAMO–RQ) furnishes DA-approved D–Rates to ODCSLOG (DALO–SM).

(2) ODCSLOG forwards the distribution rates to DESCOM where the rates are applied to the appropriate fiscal year LOGSACS file/computer tape to include the deployment sequence for determining ammunition stockage levels. The LOGSACS file/computer tape will basically be the same one used by CAA in their computation of the D–Rates.

(3) An ARSTAF committee chaired by ODCSOPS (DAMO–RQ) reviews the distribution rates to determine those ammunition items which may require a change in rate due to changes in force structure, threat, scenario, etc.

(4) Promulgated distribution rates are published in Supply Bulletin 38–26 (DALO–SM).

4–4. Training ammunition requirements.

a. References. AR 350–1, dated 25 April 1975, and AR 350–4, dated 24 September 1973.

b. Definitions.

(1) *Training ammunition.* Supply Class V items consumed during training. It includes both training-unique and service ammunition, explosives and pyrotechnics. It does not include ammunition expended for purposes other than training such as—

(a) Research, development, test, and evaluation (developmental and user testing).

(b) Disposal.

(c) Environmental hazard control.

(d) Military interments.

(e) Saluting.

(f) State security.

(g) Weapons calibration and test.

(h) Wildlife protection.

(i) Guard duty.

(j) Emergency signals.

(k) Law enforcement.

(l) Rock quarry operations.

(m) Road repairs and construction.

(n) Other activities even though incidental training value may be gained.

(2) *Training-unique ammunition.* Ammunition which has no battlefield use and is procured solely for the purpose of training.

(3) *Training Ammunition Management System (TAMS)(AR 5–13).* A comprehensive system for the management of

training ammunition focusing on the determination of requirements and efficient management of authorizations. TAMS is designed to operate within the framework of the Planning, Programing, and Budgeting System.

(4) *The Training Ammunition Authorization Committee (TAAC).* A continuing standing committee of the Department of the Army organized under the provisions of AR 15–20, composed of senior representatives of the Army Staff and major commands. Its purpose is to validate Army training ammunition requirements and to make recommendations to DCSOPS concerning their incorporation into ammunition procurement programs.

c. Procedure.

(1) Initial guidance regarding training goals and draft training ammunition authorizations will be provided by HQDA in Program and Budget Guidance (PBG).

(2) MACOMs and the Army National Guard (ARNG) present proposed requirements to the TAAC. The TAAC will consider training ammunition requirements and address the impact of shortfalls on the attainment of training goals. TAAC-validated requirements will form the basis for training ammunition input into the Army Materiel Plan (AMP).

(3) MACOMs which participate in the programing cycle may submit their unsatisfied ammunition requirements for the first year of the five program years in their Program Analysis and Resource Review (PARR). These PARR issues are reviewed by the Army Staff and presented through the Program Budget Committee (PBC) and Select Committee (SELCOM) to the CSA and SA for review and approval.

(4) The POM is prepared concurrently with the program review and approval process and includes the training ammunition program. As ammunition procurement programs are modified by the formulation of the OSD and President's Budget, and congressional action, draft ammunition authorizations will be provided MACOMs and the ARNG for further review.

(5) If complete funding of training ammunition programs is not provided, ODCSOPS, in coordination with ODCSLOG and ODCSRDA, will determine the amount that war reserve stocks can be drawn down to satisfy training needs without unacceptable degradation of force readiness. Such war reserve assets may be applied against unfunded training ammunition requirements.

(6) Prior to the beginning of the fiscal year, the TAAC will meet to consider requirements and budget decisions on the Army Materiel Program. Final MACOM and ARNG authorizations for the budget year will be made. MACOMs and the ARNG will subauthorize to elements of their commands and the several states, respectively, in accordance with DA guidance, MACOM and ARNG determination of priorities, needs, and local conditions. The subauthorization process will continue to unit level.

(7) Requirements for training-unique ammunition to support Reserve component unit training subsequent to mobilization and prior to deployment are developed by FORSCOM and the ARNG, approved by ODCSOPS, and furnished to ODCSRDA for inclusion in annual procurement requirements.

(8) Unless prohibited or restricted by command or ARNG policy, any commander may adjust the ammunition authorization for his command to meet the needs of his training program provided only that—

(a) the total dollar value of the authorization is not exceeded and

(b) the change is supportable from the ammunition stockpile. The dollar value of authorizations and individual ammunition items will be included within the TAMIS data base. Annual authorizations to MACOMs and the ARNG may include a permissible quantity by which authorizations of individual items may be increased without DA approval. This quantity will be based on a comparison of asset posture and operational war reserve requirements.

(9) Supplemental authorizations to MACOMs and the ARNG may be approved by HQDA to meet onetime requirements which cannot be supported from within existing authorizations and are essential to the furtherance of the MACOM or ARNG mission. Normally such supplemental authorizations will be approved only when the requirement supports an HQDA directed tasking made subsequent to the approval of annual authorizations.

(10) Ammunition items experiencing, or forecast to experience, demands exceeding supply availability will be allocated, distributed, and/or redistributed by the Committee for Ammunition Logistical Support (CALS) in accordance with AR 15–16.

d. Responsibilities.

(1) ODCSOPS is responsible for the overall management of training ammunition and TAMS (DAMO–TRS); monitoring the overall ammunition system to ensure integration of all requirements and the assignment of appropriate priorities (DALO–RQR); defending the funding of training requirements (DAMO–TRS); assessing, in coordination with ODCSLOG and ODCSRDA, whether war reserve stocks can be drawn down to satisfy training ammunition requirements without unacceptable degradation of force readiness (DALO–RQL); and establishing priorities between competing claimants when training ammunition authorizations and/or availability are less than requirements (DAMO–TRS).

(2) ODCSLOG is responsible for policy formulation regarding maintenance, care, renovation, and distribution of training ammunition.

(3) ODCSRDA is responsible for the development and defense of ammunition procurement programs; overall management of a research and development program that will facilitate the fielding of systems, training devices, simulators, and training-unique items to enhance training; and providing ODCSOPS with information on procurement

programs and assets to enable ODCSOPS to assess if contingency stocks can be drawn down to satisfy training ammunition requirements, or if additional procurement should be considered.

(4) FORSCOM is responsible for the determination of training unique ammunition requirements for post-mobilization/predeployment training.

4–5. War reserve stocks for allies.

a. Reference. AR 11–11(C), Army Programs, War Reserves(U), 1 February 1979 (under revision).

b. Definition. War Reserve Stocks for Allies (WRSA). WRSA consists of OSD-directed programs to ensure US preparedness to assist specific allied countries in the event of war. WRSA remain US owned and controlled until transferred in accordance with the Foreign Assistance Act of 1961 and International Security Assistance Acts, as amended. The WRSA is based on guidance from the Secretary of Defense as implemented by HQDA.

c. Concept. ODCSOPS provides the HQDA-approved force structure and weapons densities to be supported to ODCSRDA and ODCSLOG. ODCSRDA and ODCSLOG compute munitions programing and distribution requirements based on the number of days to be supported as specified in OSD guidance. This gross requirement is then reduced (offset) by the allied countries' assets applicable to war reserve. This net requirement becomes the WRSA portion of the US total AAO.

d. Responsibilities.

(1) *ODCSOPS—*

(a) Has primary responsibility for preparing and coordinating the overall WRSA program.

(b) Annually revalidates the supported allied force structure, the type items, and quantities by line item that are to be supported and forwards the validated list to ODCSLOG, ODCSRDA, and DARCOM.

(c) Prescribes ammunition rates to be used.

(d) Establishes programing priorities for WRSA Program in the DA Programing Priorities List (DAPPL) and Army priorities for programing.

(e) Establishes distribution priorities for WRSA Program in the DA Master Priority List (DAMPL).

(2) *ODCSLOG—*

(a) Assists in the validation of WRSA.

(b) Distributes ammunition assets to WRSA in accordance with Department of the Army Master Priority List/Department of the Army Program Priority List (DAMPL/DAPPL).

(c) Maintains status of WRSA assets in accordance with OSD and Army guidance.

(d) Develops requests for ceilings to be used to add ammunition to WRSA.

(3) *ODCSRDA—*

(a) Computes WRSA requirements and incorporates in the AAO, and plans, programs, and budgets PAA based on OSD and Army guidance.

(b) Assists in WRSA requirements computations and the validation of WRSA.

(4) *WRSA Review and Validation Committee—*

(a) Meets annually to validate the allied force structure and supported items and submits to ODCSOPS for approval and forwarding to ODCSLOG, ODCSRDA, and DARCOM.

(b) The committee consists of a representative from ODCSOPS (chairperson), ODCSLOG, ODCSRDA, OTSG, and OCSA(PA&E) with representation from EUSA, WESTCOM, DARCOM, OACSI, OCA, and OCE when requested by committee chairperson.

(c) The committee will meet at the call of the chairperson.

4–6. Special contingency stockpile.

a. Reference. AR 11–11(C), Army Programs, War Reserves(U), 15 January 1982.

b. Definitions.

(1) Special contingency stockpile. A CONUS stockpile to meet urgent unforeseen security assistance requirements. Special contingency stockpile remains US owned and controlled until transferred under the Foreign Assistance and International Security Assistance Acts.

(2) The special contingency stockpile is based on guidance from the Secretary of Defense as implemented by HQDA.

c. Concept.

(1) For items for which there is a specified daily consumption rate, that figure times the specified support period equals the requirement.

(2) For items for which there is no specified daily consumption, the US NATO 90–day intense rate times the weapons density times the specified support period is used to compute the requirement.

d. Responsibilities.

(1) *ODCSOPS—*

(a) Has primary responsibility for preparing and coordinating the overall SCS Program.

(b) Annually revalidates special contingency stockpile ammunition items and forwards stockage level to ODCSLOG, ODCSRDA, and DARCOM.

(c) Computes the required special contingency stockpile ammunition levels in accordance with OSD and Army guidance. Prescribes ammunition rates to be used.

(d) Establishes programing priorities for SCS Program in DAPPL and Army priorities for programing.

(e) Establishes distribution priorities for SCS Program in DAMPL.

(2) *ODCSLOG*—

(a) Assists in the validation of special contingency stockpile.

(b) Distributes ammunition assets to special contingency stockpile in accordance with DAMPL/DAPPL.

(c) Maintains status of special contingency stockpile assets in accordance with OSD and Army guidance.

(3) *ODCSRDA*—

(a) Incorporates special contingency stockpile requirements into the AAO, and plans, programs and budgets Procurement of Ammunition, Army Appropriation based on OSD and Army guidance.

(b) Assists in special contingency stockpile requirements computations and the validation of the special contingency stockpile.

(4) *WRSA Review and Validation Committee*— Meets annually to validate the special contingency stockpile stockage requirement and submit it to DCSOPS for approval and forwarding to ODCSLOG, ODCSRDA, and DARCOM.

4–7. Operational projects (non-POMCUS).

a. *Reference.* Change 14, AR 710–1, dated 12 April 1976.

b. *Definitions.*

(1) *Operational project.* An authorization for major commanders to acquire materiel for theater or CONUS stockage for the purpose of supporting specific operations, contingencies, and/or war plans.

(2) *Additive project.* Projects which consist of requirements in addition to initial issue allowances (MTOE, TDA, MTDA, and CTA). Additive projects automatically increase the AAO by the project quantities.

(3) *Nonadditive projects.* Projects which do not increase materiel acquisition objectives and are included in a Modification Table of Organization and Equipment (MTOE), Tables of Distribution and Allowances/Modification Table of Distribution and Allowances (TDA/MTDA), and common table of allowances (CTA).

(4) *Proponent.* An activity or agency which proposes an operational project and which is responsible for controlling and reporting the materiel required for the project.

(5) *Project section.* A subdivision or part of a complete operational project with separate areas of operation or different degrees of use or project implementation.

c. *Policy.*

(1) Operational projects are to support the requirements of major Army commanders for special needs over and above normal allowances.

(2) Initiators will take appropriate action to satisfy operational project requirements from existing authorizations, such as Theater War Reserves (AR 11–11) or other operational projects prior to requesting additional operational project authorizations.

(3) Materiel requirements for support of contingencies, civil relief, disturbances, or defense not otherwise covered by ARs will be determined by the major commanders in the area of operations.

(4) Guidance on the use of operational project stocks to meet peacetime requirements is contained in section II of chapter 8 of AR 710–1. Peacetime use of an operational project may occur only after DA approval (ODCSLOG).

d. *Establishment of operational projects.*

(1) The proponent of an operational project may be any MACOM, activity, or agency.

(2) Maximum coordination will be conducted between MACOM, Item Managers, and the Army Staff.

(3) To initiate or change a non-POMCUS operational project proponents will (AR 710–1, para 8–27)—

(a) Prepare a request (with justification letter) for establishment of a new project or change to an existing project.

(b) Prepare an Operational Project List of Items.

(c) Submit operational project proposal to DA and DARCOM jointly.

(d) At time of submission of a new or revised operational project, the proponents are authorized to establish a holding account for materiel available within the command which can be applied to the project.

e. *ODCSLOG will—*

(1) Provide staff guidance for review and approval of all DA operational projects in coordination with ODCSOPS (DAMO–OD).

(2) Coordinate operational projects and changes with the Army staff.

(3) Advise MACOM's of project disapproval or suspension.

(4) After DARCOM processing, staff and forward approved project to TAG for publication.

(5) Annually publish HQDA letter listing all authorized operational projects providing the Army Staff and MACOM's with the listing of all additive and nonadditive projects by reflecting "A," or "N," respectively.

f. HQ DARCOM will—

(1) Review all logistical aspects of the justification letter and proposed Letter of Instruction (LOI) for proposed or revised operational projects.

(2) Provide guidance to subordinate activities on project processing.

(3) Provide management information data to HQDA.

(4) Incorporate and consider approved operational projects in the DARCOM OPLANS developed to support contingency operations.

(5) Provide project codes to the US Army Equipment Authorizations Review Activity (USAEARA), as required.

(6) Submit overall analysis of the project proposal/change to HQDA for approval.

g. Funding. Funding for non-POMCUS operational projects is as set forth in the principal Item and Ammunition Portion—Policy and Guidance for Preparation of Part I of the AMP. Proponents requiring stocks for approved operational projects will budget and provide funds for supplies and equipment.

h. Stocks no longer required. When project stocks are no longer required, proponents will forward a letter to HQDA with a copy to HQ DARCOM requesting that the project be canceled.

Chapter 5
OTHER CUSTOMER SUPPORT

5–1. US customers.

a. Under the authority of the Secretary of Defense, the Secretary of the Army is assigned as the Single Manager for Conventional Ammunition (SMCA) within the Department of Defense with power to redelegate, within the Army, those authorities for performance of this function. The current organizational structure is portrayed in figure 5–1.

b. The US Army acts as the procurement agent for most munitions used commonly by the several DOD services plus many items used by only one service, and for foreign customers under security assistance programs.

c. Under the SMCA, the requirements for all Services and customers are aggregated. Budgeting is the responsibility of the separate services. Military Interdepartmental Purchase Requests (MIPR's) are submitted to the SMCA to procure the customer orders. Deliveries are made to the customer as stocks are produced, or the stocks are placed in storage under the SMCA custodial management.

d. Because the ammunition production base for many items is common to all services, this base must satisfy joint service peacetime requirements and also be able to expand to accommodate mobilization requirements for all services.

e. While there has been contact between services to dispose of the potential excess of one service and avoid unneeded procurements by others, there was no mechanism to identify a local need for one service to assets available in nearby storage belonging to another service.

f. Under the SMCA, the mechanism now exists and extensive savings of second destination transportation funds are made possible by avoiding cross-hauling of stocks.

g. Support by the SMCA requires that funding programs related to care, preservation, storage, management, and maintenance of the production base for conventional ammunition support the ammunition procurement programs and ammunition readiness for all customers.

h. The SMCA also supports the Treasury Department, Department of the Interior (avalanche control), and the Immigration Service Border Patrol. These requirements are generally received as funded requisitions. Army stock is maintained by replacement procurement orders.

5–2. Security assistance programs.

a. Security Assistance Programs, Military Assistance Program (MAP), and Foreign Military Sales (FMS) provide a source for other nations to acquire equipment and munitions for national defense without commitment of large capital outlay to a defense industrial base. These programs provide the basis for international mutual support and can be an effective element of US foreign policy implementation.

b. Security assistance requirements provide one means for maintenance of an active, prepared production base for combat-essential items currently not needed by the US in quantities sufficient to maintain production continuity. Additionally, certain economies related to production continuity help to reduce hardware unit costs.

c. Security assistance requirements also provide a means for disposal of stocks no longer needed in the US inventory. In addition to reduced storage costs, the cost of demilitarization is avoided,

5–3. Protection of US Stocks to ensure readiness.

a. The objective is to provide support to security assistance programs and other US customers while maintaining an adequate state of ammunition supply readiness.

b. To obtain these ends, it is essential that other customer requirements which are proposed for shipment from Army ammunition stock shall not reduce those stock levels below the greater of the Army Procurement or Distribution Objective unless an exception to policy is approved by ODCSOPS.

c. When another customer requirement, or a combination of requirements, will reduce Army stocks below the levels stated above, customer orders shall be furnished from procurement sources using normal leadtime unless otherwise approved by ODCSOPS, or other appropriate authority.

● Secretary of the Army

(Assigned as SMCA by DOD Directive 5160.65)

● Assistant Secretary of Army (RDA)

(Assigned SMCA policy matters by SMCA Charter)

● Deputy Chief of Staff for Research, Development and Acquisition

(Assigned as the central focal point for integration and coordination of SMCA actions within the DA staff by SMCA Charter)

● Commanding General, US Army Materiel Development and Readiness Command

(Delegated by SMCA Charter the authorities of the Secretary of Army for execution of SMCA operations with power to redelegate)

● Executive Director for Conventional Ammunition (EDCA)

(Designated by CG, DARCOM and SMCA Charter for performance of the SMCA activities with power to carry out authorities assigned to the CG, DARCOM)

● Commanding General, US Army Armament Materiel Readiness Command

(Delegated responsibility for the conduct of field operations for the SMCA by EDCA mission statement)

Figure 5-1. Single Manager for Conventional Ammunition (SMCA) Organizational Structure

5–4. Explosive ordnance disposal support.

a. Background. The mission of EOD, as outlined in AR 75–14/75–15, is to neutralize suspected or actual conventional, nuclear, chemical, biological, or improvised munitions items which have failed to function as designed or have otherwise become hazardous through damage or deterioration, and which present a threat to operations, installations, personnel, or materiel. Rendering safe and disposal may take many different forms, dependent on the location, size, and quantity, and condition of the munitions involved. US Army EOD personnel are trained to neutralize domestic as well as foreign munitions.

b. CONUS. The Department of the Army has delegated complete operational responsibility to HQ FORSCOM. HQ FORSCOM provides geographical coverage of CONUS with 50 EOD units positioned around the country. In CONUS, approximately one team per 3.5 million people or for each 85,000 square miles is used for peacetime staffing. Army EOD support is provided to all Army organizations, all DOD components and Federal, State, and local government on a 24-hour basis. HQ DARCOM has delegated all responsibilities for EOD tools, equipment, and publications to HQ ARRADCOM.

c. Theater responsibilities. Each MACOM has responsibilities to staff its command to handle EOD responsibilities. EOD units are recommended for every 30,000 US troops in the theater of operation during peacetime and additional units during wartime.

5–5. Rationalization, Standardization, and Interoperability.

a. General. Rationalization, Standardization, and Interoperability (RSI) programs and initiatives are governed primarily by AR 34–1 and AR 34–2. RSI is viewed as a means of increasing the capability of US and allied armies through the use of combined and integrated alliance resources to further national and alliance goals. As such, RSI programs and initiatives represent a commitment by the US Army to actions enhancing its own abilities to operate effectively within an alliance. The NATO Standardization Agreements (STANAGs) dealing with ammunition interoperability are listed in figure 5–2. In addition, there is an ABCA (America, Britain, Canada, Australia) Quadripartite Standardization Agreement (QSTAG) on 105mm tank gun ammunition (and cannon) as well as a Memorandum of Understanding, 31 March 1978, concerning 155mm ammunition (and cannon) for the quadrilateral countries (US, UK, FRG, and Italy). An advisory publication, ABCA Armies' Logistics Handbook—Part II, Catalogue of Common User Items of Combat Supplies, provides listings of common ammunition in chapter 5. Included in this publication is an acceptability matrix for ammunition between the ABCA Armies.

STANAG number	Subject
2002	Marking of Contaminated or Dangerous Land Areas
2034	Ammunition Supply Procedures
2143	Explosive Ordnance Reconnaissance/Explosive Ordnance Disposal (EOR/EOD)
2310	Small Arms Ammunition (7.62mm)
2316	Marking of Ammunition (Below 20mm)
2318	Charger for NATO 7.62mm Ammunition
2321	Ammunition Color Codes (20mm and above)
2322	Minimum Markings for the Identification of Ammunition
2329	Links for Use with NATO 7.62mm Cartridges
2818	Demolition Accessories
2928*	Land Forces Ammunition Interchangeability Catalogue (AOP-6)
3585	20mm Ammunition for M61 Weapons
4100	Ballistic Surveillance of Gun Ammunition
4136	20mm Ammunition for Cannon M139 (Hispano Suiza)

*Interoperability is limited to NATO Land Forces, in Emergency, in War.

Note. See AAP-4, Standardization Agreements and Allied Publications, for a complete listing of STANAG's and dates of latest editions and amendments.

Figure 5-2. Life Cycle of a Typical Round of Conventional Ammunition

b. North Atlantic Treaty Organization (NATO).

(1) The interoperability and standardization of ammunition within NATO is critically important to the improvement of operational capability, force flexibility, sustainability, and simplification of the logistic system. Dramatic progress has been made in certifying small arms, artillery, mortar, and tank gun ammunition for firing from US and allied weapons. The Army Ammunition Interoperability Plan (AAIP) was approved by the Department of the Army (DA) on 12 July 1979 which represented the first step toward the achievement of ammunition interoperability. The Army's initial efforts began in the summer of 1977 following a request from the Commander in Chief, the US Army Europe (CINCUSAREUR). Concurrently, the Joint Chiefs of Staff (JCS) identified NATO ammunition interoperability as the #2 and #3 priority goals for US forces in recognition that ammunition is the high tonnage component relative to resupply. In order to implement this plan, a prioritized methodology was formulated which allows a quick but thorough look at the specific tasks of the plan, while simultaneously initiating a close liaison effort among the developer, user, and logistics counterparts of our NATO allies.

(2) The specific methodology developed for training ammunition involved engineering analysis of all pertinent data available as a prerequisite to the establishment of a written Memorandum of Agreement (see figure 5-3 for MOA summary) between the US and individual NATO allies which would allow the interchange of ammunition during training exercises.

(3) The approach developed for combat is somewhat different. Using the appropriate Standard NATO Agreements (STANAGs) as the basis, the data are being updated, expanded into a 5-year plan, firing restrictions added and fire control information identified. These actions are designed to reevaluate and reduce many of the caveats associated with classifying ammunition stocks as condition code N, suitable for emergency combat. STANAG 2928, Land Forces Ammunition Interchangeability Catalogue (AOP-6) provides a guide for combat interchangeability of ammunition among NATO countries.

(4) The basic criterion for both training and combat is to disseminate the information to the user in the form of field manuals, technical bulletins, firing tables, and additions to computerized fire control systems. To date exchange firings have been conducted with the Federal Republic of Germany (GE) involving the 203mm howitzer. Additionally, a NATO Ammunition Interoperability Review (NAIR) has been drafted and submitted to the June 1980 Conference of National Armament Directors (CNAD). Individual NATO member countries are currently reviewing the NAIR.

US[2]	155mm	175mm	203mm	81mm	4.2"	105mm Tank
GE	X	X[3]	X			X
UK	X	X	X	X		X
CA	X			X		X
NL	X		X		X	
BE	X		X		X	X
FR	X					
NOR	X				X	X

Notes.

1. Other MOAs with Denmark, Italy, and Turkey are also under consideration.
2. For selected rounds.
3. Not interchangeable.

Figure 5.3. MOA status between US and NATO [1]allies.

c. ABCA initiatives. Each of the ABCA armies maintains standardization representatives in the other three countries actively monitoring ammunition/weapons developments and providing for flow of information between the members. Information matters considered for standardization and data on standardization hats may be routed through the standardization representative to the other ABCA countries to keep them apprised of R&D activities, to solicit comments, and to determine if a cooperative venture is desired. Subsequently, a request may be expressed for information, or there may be independent efforts going on in two or more countries and information may be exchanged on a coordinated basis, or a cooperative venture may result. In the ideal case, from a standardization viewpoint, there may be a desire to purchase another nation's weapon system, ammunition, or TDP. Usually one of the foregoing RSI efforts requires negotiation and subsequent approval in one form or another. Some of the more important existing or proposed agreements related to ammunition are listed in figure 5–4. A complete listing may be found in the ABC Armies Standardization Lists.

d. Production capability. In general, it is well known that some of our allies have the capabilities to produce US-designed ammunition. However, complete details are not available, nor is it positively known that those foreign countries which can produce, and are producing, to US designs, are doing so in strict conformance with the US TDP.

Name of project	ABCA control number	Developing Army	Interested Armies	Type of Coop R&D	Date on list	Remarks
155mm Cannon-Launched Guided Projectile (CLGP) (COPPERHEAD)	1-1-1-31	US	UK	Interdependent	1973	Signed UK/US MOU
			CA	Interdependent		
Project No. 1X664621D073			AS	Interdependent		
Ammo for Cannon 155mm Howitzer	1-1-1-32	US	CA	Interdependent	1974	
Project No. 1X664602D373			AS	Interdependent		
155mm Ammunition for Artillery Weapons	1-1-1-40	US/ UK	US/ UK	Coordination	1974	Signed Quadripartite Ballistics Agreement (US/UK/FRG/IT)
Improved Screening Smoke Cartridge for the 81mm Mortar (LOA)	1-1-6-3	US	CA	Interdependent	Dec 77	
External Ammunition Stores Management and Remote-Controlled Fuzing Subsystems for Attack Helicopters (ROC)	1-5-3	US	US	Interdependent		Provisionally entered on Stan List, Part 1. UK has bid for Interdependent R&D.
2.75-Inch Rocket Lightweight Launcher and Improved External Stores Rack (ROC)	1-5-3-	US	UK	Interdependent		US has yet to confirm this course.
2.75-Inch Rocket Smoke Warhead (ROC)	1-5-3-	US	UK	Interdependent		

Figure 5-4. Data Extracted from ABCA Armies Standardization Lists—Part 1—Cooperative R&D.

Appendix A
REFERENCES

A–1. Department of Defense regulations.
  a. DOD Directive 5000.1, Major System Acquisition, 29 March 1982.

  b. DOD Instruction 5000.2, Major System Acquisition Procedures, 19 March 1980.

  c. DOD Directive 5154.4, The DOD Explosive Safety Board (DDESB), 24 January 1978.

  d. DOD Directive 5160.65, Single Manager for Conventional Ammunition, 17 November 1981.

  e. DOD Approved SMCA Charter, 26 February 1982.

A–2. Army regulations.
  a. AR 5–13, Management: Training Ammunition Management System, 1 August 1979.

  b. AR 10–5, Organizations and Functions: Department of the Army, 1 December 1980.

  c. AR 10–11, Organizations and Functions: US Army Materiel Development and Readiness Command, 9 March 1977.

  d. AR 10–41, Organizations and Functions: US Army Training and Doctrine Command, 27 June 1973.

  e. AR 10–42, Organizations and Functions: US Army Forces Command, 15 April 1975.

  f. (C) AR 11–11, Army Programs: War Reserves, 15 January 1982. (Downgraded from (S) to (C) by HQDA (DALO–SMW) message 131504Z Jun 80.)

  g. AR 11–27, Army Programs: Army Energy Program, 20 July 1976.

  h. AR 15–2, Boards, Commissions, and Committees: Department of the Army Allocation Committee, Ammunition (DAACA), 12 August 1968.

  i. AR 15–16, Boards, Commissions, and Committees: Department of the Army Committee for Ammunition Logistic Support (CALS), 23 October 1974.

  j. AR 15–20, Boards, Commissions, and Committees: Training Ammunition Authorization Committee, 8 February 1977.

  k. AR 34–1, Standardization: US Army Participation in Internal Military Rationalization, Standardization and Interoperability (RSI) Programs, 15 October 1979.

  l. AR 34–2, Standardization: Rationalization, Standardization, and Interoperability, 15 December 1980.

  m. AR 55–355, Transportation and Travel: Military Traffic Management Regulation, 15 March 1969, with changes.

  n. AR 70–1, Research, Development and Acquisition: Army Research, Development, and Acquisition, 1 May 1975, with change.

  o. AR 70–10, Research and Development: Test and Evaluation During Development and Acquisition of Materiel, 29 August 1975.

  p. AR 70–27, Research and Development: Outline Development Plan/ADM/DPM/DCP, 17 March 1975.

  q. AR 70–41, Research and Development: Cooperation with Allies and other Nations in Research and Development of Defense Equipment, 1 June 1981.

  r. AR 70–61, Research, Development and Acquisition: Type Classification of Army Materiel, 1 August 1978.

  s. AR 71–2, Force Development: Basis of Issue Plans, 19 April 1976.

  t. AR 71–3, Force Development: User Testing, 8 March 1977.

  u. AR 71–9, Force Development: Materiel Objectives and Requirements (under revision: Final Draft 26 February 1981).

  v. AR 75–14, Explosives: Interservice Responsibilities for Explosive Ordnance Disposal, 25 September 1973.

  w. AR 75–15, Explosives: Responsibilities and Procedures for Explosive Ordnance Disposal, 1 November 1978.

  x. AR 130–5, Army National Guard: Organization and Functions of National Guard Bureau, 8 December 1977.

  y. AR 130–400, Army National Guard: Logistical Policies for Support, 5 January 1977.

  z. AR 200–1, Environmental Quality: Environmental Protection and Enhancement, 20 January 1978.

  aa. AR 220–1, Field Organizations: Unit Status Reporting (RCS JCS 6–11–2–1–6), 1 June 1981.

  ab. AR 350–1, Training: Army Training, 1 August 1981.

  ac. AR 350–4, Training: Qualification and Familiarization with Weapons and Weapons Systems, 24 September 1973.

  ad. AR 350–6, Training: Army-Wide Small Arm Competitive Marksmanship, 26 February 1974.

  ae. AR 350–35, Training: New Equipment Training and Introduction, 1 November 1981.

  af. AR 700–20, Logistics: Ammunition Peculiar Equipment (APE), 15 April 1979.

  ag. AR 700–22, Logistics: Worldwide Ammunition Reporting System (WARS); RCS (GSGLD–1322) (R1)(MIN), 18 August 1976 (under revision).

  ah. AR 700–90, Logistics: Army Industrial Preparedness Program, 15 April 1982.

  ai. AR 700–127, Logistics: Integrated Logistic Support, 1 April 1981.

aj. AR 702–6, Product Assurance: Ammunition Stockpile Reliability Program (ASRP), 1 June 1980.

ak. AR 702–9, Product Assurance: Product Testing of Army Materiel, 7 March 1977.

al. AR 710–1, Inventory Management: Centralized Inventory Management of the Army Supply System, 30 December 1970, with changes.

am. AR 710–2, Inventory Management: Materiel Management for Using Units Support Units, and Installations, 1 October 1981.

an. AR 710–8, Inventory Management: Non-nuclear Ammunition Combat Rates, 3 January 1975.

ao. AR 740–1, Storage and Supply Activities: Storage and Supply Activity Operations, 23 April 1971, with changes.

ap. AR 740–26, Storage and Supply Activities: Physical Inventory Control, 1 July 1980.

aq. AR 750–1, Maintenance of Supplies and Equipment: Army Materiel Maintenance Concepts and Policies, 1 April 1978, with changes.

ar. AR 1000–1, Utilization: Basic Policies for Systems Acquisition, 1 May 1980 (under revision).

A–3. Chief of Staff regulations (Apply only to HQDA).

a. CSR 5–13, Management: Ammunition Management, 13 January 1981.

b. CSR 10–20, Organization and Functions: Office of the Deputy Chief of Staff for Operations and Plans (under revision).

c. CSR 10–21, Organization and Functions: Office of the Deputy Chief of Staff for Personnel, 17 August 1978.

d. CSR 10–22, Organization and Functions: Office of the Deputy Chief of Staff for Logistics, 6 November 1979.

e. CSR 10–24, Organization and Functions: Office of the Deputy Chief of Staff for Research, Development, and Acquisition, 18 January 1980.

f. CSR 11–1, Army Programs: The Planning, Programing, and Budgeting System, 25 November 1974.

g. (C) CSR 11–21, Army Programs: Review and Approval of War Reserve Stock, Allies (WRSA) and Contingency Stockpile (SCS) Program (U) 17 January 1979.

A–4. Other publications.

a. (C) SB 38–26, Logistics Management: Non-nuclear Ammunition Supply Rates (U), 20 April 1979.

b. TM 38–750, Logistics Management: The Army Maintenance Management System (TAMMS), 31 May 1981.

c. TM 43–0001–28, Army Ammunition Data Sheets: Artillery Ammunition, 25 April 1977, with changes.

Appendix B
MANAGEMENT INFORMATION SYSTEMS

B–1. Army Ammunition Management Information Systems.
Management Information Systems which support Army ammunition management include the following:

a. Worldwide Ammunition Reporting System (WARS).

b. Conventional Ammunition Readiness Evaluation System (CARES).

c. Standard Army Ammunition System (SAAS).

(1) Theater Applications—level 1.

(2) Below Theater Application—level 3 (not currently operational).

(3) Storage Activity—level 4 (not currently operational).

d. Standard USAREUR Munitions Systems (SUMS).

e. USARJ Standard Ammunition System.

f. Korea Ammunition Management System (KAMS).

g. Installation Worldwide Ammunition Reporting System (IWARS).

h. MACOM Worldwide Ammunition Reporting System (MWARS).

i. Training Ammunition Management Information System (TAMIS).

j. Structure and Composition System (SACS).

k. Production Base Plans and Management Systems.

B–2. Worldwide Ammunition Reporting System (WARS).
Logistics management information system used by ammunition managers throughout the Army at all management echelons. The system consists of the following four subsystem modules:

- Requirements and Assets.
- Maintenance, Renovation, and Demilitarization.
- Serviceability.
- Readiness Assessment.

a. The focus of the system is the Department of Army Ammunition Management Information Data Bank operated by the ARRCOM. That data bank, with one or two exceptions, is the source of the WARS reports. The exceptions are those reports which are executed on a manual basis, such as the Allocation Report and the Toxic Chemical Munitions Report.

b. The WARS Data Bank receives feeder reports from a series of standard systems; these are—

- The DARCOM Commodity Command Standard System.
- The DARCOM Depot Standard System Application (SSA).
- SAAS.
- The FORSCOM/TRADOC Feeder Systems (MWARS).

c. The following are outputs of the modules indicated and their frequency:

(1) *Part 1. Worldwide Ammunition Requirements and Assets Reports.*

(a) Monthly . . . . M

(b) Quarterly . . . . Q

(c) Tonnage/Cost Data . . . . Q

(d) Maintenance & Packaging Materiel . . . . Q

(e) Toxic Chemical Agents . . . . S/A

(f) Dummy Drill & Inert . . . . A

(g) Allocations . . . . S/A

(h) Training Authorization/Expenditure . . . . Q

(2) *Part II. Worldwide Ammunition Maintenance Reports.*

(a) Renovation/Packaging & Preservation . . . . M

(b) Demilitarization/Disposal . . . . M

(3) *Part III. Worldwide Ammunition Serviceability Report.*
(Inspection and Lot Number)

(a) DODIC, NSN, Lot Number by Location . . . . Q

(b) DODIC, NSN, Lot Number Consolidated Report . . . . Q

(c) DODIC, NSN, Lot Number Suspensions/Restrictions . . . . Q

(d) Analysis of unserviceable assets by condition code, NSN, and Lot Number . . . . Q

B–3. Conventional Ammunition Readiness Evaluation System (CARES).

a. The purpose of CARES is to access conventional ammunition readiness by timing increment from M–day to M+180 days in three situations:

(1) 180 days of combat support in Europe.

(2) 180 days of combat support in the Pacific (Korea).

(3) A worst case combination of (1) and (2) above.

b. CARES uses existing data bases including WARS for assets and DESCOM D–Rate Computations (based on AR 11–11) for combat requirements. CARES then performs a readiness assessment for each item of ammunition (by DODAQ based on days of supply to the requirement based on the following criteria (see AR 720–1):

(1) C1 if stock availability to meet requirement is 90 percent or greater.

(2) C2 if 80 percent but less than 90 percent.

(3) C3 if 65 percent but less than 80 percent.

(4) C4 if less than 65 percent. CARES summary data can also be displayed by categories; i.e., small caliber, mortar, tank, artillery, etc., as required.

c. The following are outputs of CARES:

(1) Part I—displays assets by timeframe stratified to a requirement expressed in seven time periods—M–day to M+15, M+15 to M+30, and 30–day increment through M+180.

(2) Part II—Displays by DODAC the days and percent short to 180–day requirement and projected "get well" date.

(3) Readiness condition; i.e., C1, C2, C3, or C4 by DODAC.

B–4. Standard Army Ammunition System (SAAS).

a. Standard prior to 1973. Prior to 1973, the Army did not have a standard automated ammunition management system for use in the field. Operations were basically manual; however, several commands had unique ADP systems for providing class V management information and developing the WARS report for ARRCOM.

b. 1971—DA published CSM 71–202. On 1 June 1971, DA published CSM 71–202, which governed Standard Army Intermediate Level Supply (SAILS) development. The SAILS concept originally included ammunition. Subsequent to the CSM, the class V portion was withdrawn from SAILS and established as a separate element of the Standard Army Logistics System (SALS). This new system was entitled SAAS. A DA tasking letter formalizing this action was published on 11 January 1972. As a result of a DA decision to accelerate the SAAS development effort as well as to field an operational system in USAREUR as soon as possible, a detailed analysis of current ongoing systems was undertaken. The result of this analysis was the selection of the US Army Pacific (USARPAC) Central Munitions System to serve as the theater system baseline. In addition, WARS was selected as the baseline reporting system for SAAS between the major command (level 1) and the national level.

c. 1973—SAAS designated as level 1 system. In June 1973, the converted USARPAC Central Munitions System was tested by the 60th Ordnance Group, USAREUR. This system was accepted by USAREUR in July 1973, renamed SAAS, and designated as the level 1 (theater) system. At the same time, the USARPAC Central Munitions System operated by USARPAC at Fort Shafter, Hawaii, was replaced by the SAAS level 1 system.

d. Theater Application—level 1.

(1) *Level 1.* The Theater Materiel Management Center (MMC) is an activity which performs centralized theater inventory management, maintains visibility of all theater assets, and acts as the theater's interface with the DARCOM wholesale level. It performs the mission and functions of supply management, maintenance, serviceability, transportation, intransit control, and SAAS/NICP interface management. It also provides the required logistical/tactical interface management. Ammunition assets are divided into five general categories—

(a) Prepositioned War Reserve Materiel Stocks (PWRMS). These are part of the theater's war reserve and represent stockage levels of mission-essential items to support post D-day combat consumption until resupply from CONUS facilities can be accomplished.

(b) Operational project stocks. These are part of the theater's war reserve and represent operational project stocks approved in accordance with AR 710–1. These projects provide authorization for the major commander to acquire materiel in support of specific operations, contingencies, and/or plans for specific geographical areas.

(c) Basic loads. Basic load is that quantity of nonnuclear ammunition the theater commander (FORSCOM Commander for Strategic Army Forces (STRAF) Units) authorizes for wartime purposes and requires to be designated for and carried into combat by a unit. The basic load provides the unit sufficient ammunition to sustain itself in combat until the unit can be resupplied. The basic load is managed by the unit and includes, but is not necessarily limited to, ammunition carried by the individual soldier, stored in crew vehicles, carried on prime movers and in the unit trains. It is expressed in rounds, units of weight for each type ammunition for each type weapon, and in other units of measure

for bulk allotment items. Basic loads do not include items authorized by Tables of Organization and Equipment (TOE)/ Tables of Distribution and Allowances (TDA) (e.g., explosive components of sets or kits).

(d) Training/operational stocks. These stocks include ammunition required to support training requirements and other operational requirements which do not fall within the other requirement categories.

(e) Combat operations support levels. These are stock levels required for combat areas upon initial entry into conflict. The PPWR stocks become a part of these levels and are applied against the stockage objective.

(2) *Operational Status.* SAAS level 1 is operational at Fort Shafter, Hawaii. The Central Ammunition Management Office-Pacific (CAMO–PAC) performs theater level management for the US Army in the Pacific Theater. SAAS level 1 is also operational in Zweibruecken, Germany, where the 200th Theater Army MMC performs theater ammunition management for USAREUR.

e. Below Theater Application—level 3.

(1) *Level 3.* The stock control activity is an activity which exercises stock control over the assets of one or more storage activities. It is also the highest level at which formal accountability may be maintained in an automated environment. It is basically the management level which controls the operations of all its subordinate levels and provides the interface with level 1. It accomplishes supply, maintenance, serviceability, transportation, storage, in-transit control, and SAAS interface management. It also provides the required logistical/tactical interface management.

(2) *Goal.* The SAAS level 3 system will be designed to provide improved operational capabilities for the level 3 activity while minimizing manual workload. This will be accomplished by improved information processing on third generation automatic data processing equipment (ADPE) and an automated interface with other standard systems as the Army Master Data File (AMDF), Asset Control System (ACS), and Department of the Army Management Movement System (DAMMS). SAAS level 3 will provide an improved management system by performing the following functions:

(a) Processing MILSTRIP, MILSTAMP, and excess documents. Military Standard Requisitioning and Issue Procedures (MILSTRIP), Military Standard Transportation and Movement Procedures (MILSTAMP), excess and related SAAS documents will be maintained on a history file.

(b) Maintain stock status. The SAAS level 3 system will maintain stock status by only the DOD identification code (DODIC) or by a combination of DODIC, national stock number (NSN), and lot number. Flexibility will be included in the level 3 system which will enable one storage site to report stock status by DODIC while another site reports by transactions containing DODIC, NSN, and lot number. If NSN and lot number information is maintained, parallel DODIC summary information will be automatically produced for stock status reporting to SAAS level 1. Records will be maintained by account code and condition, showing quantity on hand, quantity due in, and quantity due out for each storage site.

(c) Reconciliation process. SAAS level 1 will periodically reconcile its stock balances with those stock balances at level 3. This reconciliation will be by DODIC, account, condition code, and quantity on hand. A reconciliation card is currently produced by the SAAS level 1 system. The SAAS level 3 system will be designed to accept this reconciliation card from level 1, detect any imbalances, and produce an exception report on imbalances for the level 3 manager. Adjustments necessary to correct any imbalances will be submitted by the level 3 manager during periodic stock status reporting.

(d) Maintain accountable stock records. The level 3 activity will use the detailed reporting capability described above when maintaining accountable records. Accountability may be maintained by a general support (GS) activity or any activity with centralized accountability for a number of remote storage sites. Daily or periodic (as required) receipt, issue, and adjustment transactions by DODIC, national item identification number (NHN), and lot number will be submitted to the level 3 activity by storage sites to update accountable stock balances. These transactions will be in MILSTRIP format to the maximum extent possible. All documents which update the accountable balances will be recorded on a historical file to maintain an audit trail. When accountability has been centralized at the level 3 activity, the SAAS level 3 system will produce inventory requests, Inventory/Location Survey Cards (DA Form 2000), and inventory and location survey worksheets as required by AR 710–2 and AR 740–26. In addition, the many reports required to support accountability will be produced for the level 3 manager. These reports include voucher registers, daily transaction reports, and other similar reports.

(e) Maintain serviceability information. Maintain serviceability information that will enable the level 3 activity to segregate stocks based on suspension notices and to provide lot number information for the WARS report and other management functions. Serviceability information will be maintained by DODIC, lot number, NSN, type storage code, year of manufacture, defect codes, component lot numbers, quantity on hand, and by condition codes.

(f) Guided missiles and large rockets (GMLR) asset data. The SAAS level 3 system will be designed to provide the level 3 manager with the detailed information he needs to manage GMLR items. For a complete asset picture of all items in the Level 3 area of responsibility, the SAAS level 3 system will record GMLR assets on hand at the DSU/ GSU or held by individual units. GMLR items will be recorded by unit identification code (UIC) and serial number in all circumstances. Summary information by DODIC is also maintained to facilitate conversion from peacetime to wartime environments.

(g) Compute authorized levels. The level 3 system will compute authorized levels by storage site, DODIC, and

account. The level 3 manager will have the option of designating by storage site and account the method by which the authorized level is computed.

(h) Asset stratification. The SAAS level 3 system will have the ability to stratify assets against authorized levels by account code. The level 3 manager will establish stratification parameters on the Requirements Data File and will be provided a report showing the results of the stratification (report similar to PCN–AJB–230 in the SAAS level 1 system).

(3) *Special requirements for an independent force.* Because an independent force must have the ability to rapidly deploy to remote areas, the capability will be included in the SAAS level 3 system to allow the independent forces to bypass the normal interface with a SAAS level 1 activity and interface direct with CONUS wholesale support activities.

f. Storage Activity—level 4. The storage activity is one whose principal mission is to exercise custody of stocks for distribution to the user Direct Support Unit (DSU role) or to other storage activities General Support Unit (GSU role). This is an operational level and accomplishes supply, maintenance, serviceability, transportation, and storage operations. It operates in a manual environment but may provide interface input to level 3 in a punch card format.

B–4. Standard USAREUR Munitions Systems (SUMS).

a. Background. To accommodate the installation of the SAAS level 1 system in USAREUR, the Miesau Army Depot lot locator system was renamed as the SUMS and expanded to provide a reporting capability to SAAS level 1. SUMS operates in two modes, the "depot mode" and the "visibility mode." The "depot mode" accommodates those processes necessary for managing and controlling the day-to-day operations of an accountable supply distribution activity (ASDA) such as Miesau Army Depot. (Class V accountability in USAREUR is decentralized.) This service is provided also for the 84th Ordnance Battalion in support of its management of approximately thirty (30) prestock points stocking war reserves and units basic loads. SUMS serves all other USAREUR munitions activities in the nonaccountable "visibility mode."

b. Operation. The SUMS system is based on a unit record for each ammunition lot/serial number by NSN and DODIC in a specific condition code at a location. Various reports are produced from the SUMS data base to show the status of all ammunition items in the theater. Other normal management reports such as voucher registers and edit/error lists are also produced.

B–5. USARJ Standard Ammunition Management System.

a. Background. This system is operated by HQ USARJ, Camp Zama, Japan, and provides basic stock accounting and supply management support for US-owned class V assets in Okinawa and Japan. Since this system is used to maintain accountability for US assets in Okinawa and Japan, stock status information is recorded by DODIC, NSN, and lot number. To support accountability functions, the USARJ system produces and accepts inventory and location survey transactions. To support surveillance requirements, the USARJ system generates Q1/Q2 documents in SAAS level 1 format.

b. Operation. Various management reports are produced by the system for the ammunition manager. These reports include edit/error lists, transaction registers, inventory and location survey reports, and output card listings. In addition, a monthly stock status report is produced showing the status of on-hand assets by DODIC, NSN, lot number, condition, and warehouse location. DODIC summaries are also provided on the report which reflect tonnage and dollar-value statistics by condition code.

B–6. Korea Ammunition Management System (KAMS).

This system maintains the stock control for all US-owned class V items in Korea and is also used to maintain visibility of the Republic of Korea Army (ROKA) class V assets. Since accountability for US-owned assets in Korea has been decentralized to the storage activity, the system developed by the 19th Support Command is strictly DODIC-oriented. Lot number and NSN information required for surveillance and to be reported to SAAS level 1 is reported by a separate manual reporting system. Because the system is DODIC-oriented, a simple reporting procedure was developed containing six data fields using 24 card columns of information. Backup documentation is submitted by the storage site by mail or courier for each transaction posted to the system.

B–7. Installation and MACOM Worldwide Ammunition Reporting System.

HQ FORSCOM/TRADOC MWARS consolidates and reformats respective installation input (IWARS) for submission to ARRCOM. FORSCOM MWARS output also includes National Guard asset data. Both National Guard and Army Reserve requirements data are included in the FORSCOM/TRADOC MWARS output. MWARS/IWARS identify training, basic load and operational project assets and requirements. The condition, quantity, and location of ammunition can be monitored by the MWARS. Ammunition requirements for training are forecasted for a 12-month period for planning to facilitate distribution of items in short supply. MACOMs use this information to redistribute assets between reporting activities to meet training/test requirements. Alaska and Panama report WARS data directly to ARRCOM;

however, their reports include weapons density and War Reserve data and are, therefore, classified. The Alaska and Panama WARS Reports to ARRCOM include maintenance, packaging materiel, lot number, and age data.

B–8. Training Ammunition Management Information System (TAMIS).

a. Background. The TAMIS is a management system which provides ammunition usage information on which the commander can base his decisions. The system provides the commander with the opportunity to influence the development of his ammunition authorization so that it complements the training of his command, allows flexibility in adjusting authorizations to fit changing circumstances or environments, and permits him to have complete control over authorizations to his subordinate elements. Under this system, the commander has incentives and the flexibility to conserve or use less expensive ammunition in meeting his training goals.

b. Training Ammunition Authorization Committee. The TAAC, composed of senior Army representatives from the Army Staff and major commands, meets annually to review authorized training ammunition resources, requirements, and management and authorize training ammunition resources to MACOM and NGB for the next fiscal year. MACOMs and ARNG will subauthorize resources to elements of their commands and the ARNG.

c. Operation. Units will report expenditures of ammunition in training throughout the training year. Because the system has the facility to constantly audit a commander's use of resources through maintaining a status of credits and debits, this data (maintained within the TAMIS data base) will be the foundation for the commander to adjust the ammunition authorized for his command provided: the total dollar value of the authorization is not exceeded; the change is supportable by the stockpile; and is not prohibited or restricted by command or ARNG policy.

B–9. Structure and Composition System (SACS).

a. SACS is a network of computerized data bases which display quantitative and qualitative manpower and equipment requirements and authorizations for a selected force over time.

b. ODCSOPS is the proponent of the LOGSACS system. There are four primary component data bases which contribute to the SACS computation. They are—

(1) The Force Accounting System.

(2) The Table of Organization and Equipment File.

(3) The Army Authorization Documents System.

(4) The Basis of Issue Plans.

c. The force accounting system contains the DA Master Force (M–Force) Program. The M–Force is a troop list of the current and projected force structure. It provides the following data:

(1) Unit designation; i.e., 1/503 Abn Infantry Bn.

(2) Type of unit by mission; i.e., Armor, Infantry.

(3) Geographic location and command assignment.

(4) When the unit will be activated, inactivated, or recognized.

(5) How the unit is organized, based on the appropriate authorization documents.

d. The M–Force is maintained on computer tape in order to manage forces today and to plan future actions. It contains information on the current or real world force that should exist in the current fiscal year. This force is updated periodically to reflect changes in geographical location, changes in command assignment, activations, and deactivations. It also depicts how the Army should look at the close of the budget year and its configuration carried through the POM period. It reflects the program decisions rendered by OSD by the Presidential Budget and is amended to show changes resulting from apportionment decisions. In effect, it then becomes the apportionment force.

e. The force accounting system also contains an unconstrained force which serves as Army input to the Joint Strategic Planning Document (JSPD).

f. The table of organization (TOE) file consists of prototype organizational structures displaying minimum essential personnel and equipment required for prescribed missions of each type of unit in the Army. TRADOC is the Army proponent for development of TOEs. TOEs are approved by ODCSOPS (DAMO–RQ). A magnetic tape file is maintained of all approved TOEs plus those being processed for approval. The TOE is a prototype document used primarily for study purposes. It is no longer the basis for authority for requisition of personnel and equipment by unit commanders in the field.

g. The Army Authorization Documents System (TAADS) provides the unit in the field with the tailored structure it needs to perform its mission. TAADS is sensitive to peculiar requirements of the operational environment and secondary mission tasks. It serves as the authority for requisitions from the field for personnel and equipment. TAADS is divided into two subsystems—

(1) *The modification table of organization and equipment (MTOE).* The MTOE reflects tailored personnel and equipment modifications, to include modernization items not present in the Army inventory when the prototype TOE was developed or substitute items because of asset shortages and distribution priorities.

(2) *The tables of distribution and allowances (TDA).* A file of tables of distribution and allowance documents for all augmentation, training, and post support activities. The field commander is proponent to these documents, but the

details are transcribed into the data base. The Department of the Army Staff compiles authorizations and passes them down the chain to the parent unit commander through the Vertical TAADS (VTAADS).

h. The final major SACS component is the Basis of Issue Plan (BOIP). The BOIP consists of unit requirements for new equipment items to enter the Army inventory, but not yet reflected in the TOE. TRADOC is the proponent for BOIP. When an item of equipment is known to be available for distribution within some given timeframe, but the item is not included in any TOE and MTOE, the item may be added to the file as the file "add-on" based on the BOIP. Thus, the new item could be added to specific units in accordance with planning priorities. Ultimately, the new item is added to new TOEs, dropped from the BOIP, and included directly in revised MTOEs.

i. The SACS itself is constructed from these several data sources. First, the appropriate force is selected from the Force Accounting System. This force is updated and edited to reflect prescribed constraints based on current program guidance. The updated version of the force becomes the basis for the SACS computation.

j. The TAADS tape is now overlaid on the SACS tape. The computer can be selectively instructed to omit a TAADS document for a unit projected for reorganization and to select from the TOE file the proper TOE unit document.

k. Once units have been matched with their appropriate organizational documents, the equipment add-ons from the BOIP tape are introduced to the SACS tape. When completed, the SACS tape now contains the information to display how many personnel and how much equipment will be required to man and outfit the force being studied.

l. The final step is to aggregate the requirements into the format required. Output may be magnetic tape or hard copy prints. Outputs are usually aggregated to identify—

(1) Personnel requirements/authorizations.

(2) Procurement of Ammunition, Army (PAA) requirements for ODCSRDA budget computation purposes.

(3) Distribution requirements/authorizations for ODCSLOG and DARCOM.

m. The distribution LOGSACS is further modified by joint action of ODCSLOG, ODCSOPS, and DESCOM to limit equipment or weapons availability to that known to be available for distribution within the applicable timeframe. The "real world" constraint is not applied to the LOGSACS tape used for PAA requirements; i.e., AAO computation.

B–10. Production Base Plans and Management Systems.

a. The Production Base Plan (PBP)/Production Base Analysis (PBA). The PBP/PBA is a consolidated document which serves two basic functions:

(1) The PBA is the basis of information which provides necessary justification and direction for structuring the ammunition modernization/expansion program to support mobilization in conjunction with the five-year procurement program.

(2) The PBP reflects the results of mobilization planning to satisfy mobilization requirements on an M–Day assumed to be the first day of the budget year. The PBP reflects capability shortfalls in the existing base to meet *near-term* requirements. It also provides justification for the retention, layaway, and maintenance of the reserve production base in accordance with Defense Guidance.

b. Munitions Production Base Modernization and Expansion (M&E) Plan. The M&E Plan is maintained and periodically updated as the means for documenting and controlling the total M&E effort at the project level for all Government and commercial facilities needed to support production requirements.

c. Plant Equipment Package Management Information System (PEPMIS). The PEPMIS is a centrally managed data base for all industrial plant equipment, other plant equipment, special tooling and special test equipment required to be retained in order to meet the mobilization schedule specified in the PBP. Carefully selected data elements that are required to enable Plant Equipment Package (PEP) Managers to make necessary decisions concerning each PEP are included. The data base enables the PEP Manager to—

(1) Optimally allocate the production base equipment and special tooling.

(2) Identify equipment candidates for acquisition, rehabilitation, or replacement.

(3) Assess the impact that mobilization requirement changes have on equipment assets.

(4) Assess the capability of the plant equipment package to achieve the mobilization requirement.

d. Production Base Maintenance and Layaway Data Base. The Production Base Maintenance and Layaway Data Base consists of an automated reference file of all laidaway production lines and facilities located within the industrial base and a system of networks which identify the steps necessary to reactivate a production line or support facility. The historical file establishes a complete accessible catalog of laidaway facilities. It identifies readiness status, maintenance history, response ability, and condition status. The reactivation networks identify high risk elements, constraints, and potential trouble spots. The system will portray whether a laidaway facility can produce a product in the timeframe and quantity necessary to fill mobilization demands. This technique can also be adopted to active line acceleration and surge production.

Appendix C
SUMMARY OF GOVERNMENT PRODUCTION BASE FACILITIES

C–1. Under construction.
MISSISSIPPI ARMY AMMUNITION PLANT

INSTALLATION: Mississippi AAP, Bay St. Louis, Mississippi.

OPERATOR: GOCO—Mason-Chamberlain Inc.

MISSION/CAPABILITY: Integrated production of M483A1 155mm ICM projectile. This includes manufacture of the projectile metal parts, manufacture of the cargo metal parts and load, assembly, and pack. Using the most modern advances in manufacturing methods and technology, the plant will be capable of producing 120,000 rounds per month.

INVESTMENT, SIZE, PERSONNEL, & MODERNIZATION: Three main complexes are planned for production—
a. Projectile metal parts area with over 13 acres of roof area.
b. Cargo metal parts area with approximately 6 acres of roof area.
c. The load, assemble, and pack area with over 10 acres of roof area. An additional 5 acres of roof area will house support and administrative operations. The plant is on federally owned property comprising some 13,480 acres. Projected employment on a 1–8–5 basis will be 2,000 and approximately 5,500 at maximum production. Current personnel strength is 16 Government and 195 contractor.

HISTORY: The Mississippi AAP is the first ammunition plant to be built by the Army in more than 25 years. Although in the design stage for several years, ground was broken on 8 January 1978 on the northern portion of the NASA National Space Technology Laboratories facility. Constructing and equipping of this new facility will take place through 1982 under the management of the ARRCOM Munitions Production Base Modernization Agency. From FY76 to FY82 over $440 million of modernized/expanded facilities have been constructed or are in progress.

C–2. Active facilities.
a. CRANE ARMY AMMUNITION ACTIVITY

INSTALLATION: Crane AAA, Crane, Indiana.

OPERATOR: GOGO—ARRCOM (formerly Navy).

MISSION/CAPABILITY: Load, assemble, and pack of Navy gun ammunition, Cluster Bomb Units (CBUs) (Rockeye), bombs, warheads, fuzes, propelling charges, pyrotechnics, and initiating items.

INVESTMENT, SIZE, PERSONNEL & MODERNIZATION: Estimated replacement value is approximately $500 million. There are 7.4 million square feet of SMCA facilities with approximately 11 percent devoted to industrial production with the balance to storage. There are a total of 52,000 acres of land under SMCA control. Current personnel strength is 868 Government.

HISTORY: Commissioned in December 1941, its mission was to prepare, load, renovate, receive, store, and issue all types of naval ammunition. Crane has constantly broadened its mission through the post WWII years involving itself in more complex weapons and equipment and acquiring a Weapons Quality Engineering Center and a Fleet Logistics Support Center. In 1977 ammunition production and storage facilities and related personnel were placed under the SMCA. About 2,750 personnel and 11,000 acres are still under Navy control. Facility modernization from SMCA transfer until the end of FY82 amounts to $1.9 million.

b. HAWTHORNE ARMY AMMUNITION PLANT

INSTALLATION: Hawthorne AAP, Hawthorne, Nevada.

OPERATOR: GOCO—Day, Zimmerman, and Basil, Inc. (Formerly Navy GOGO)

MISSION/CAPABILITY: Load, assemble, and pack bombs, warhead, rockets, propelling charges, CBUs, fuel air explosive (FAE), Navy gun ammunition and related fuzes, primers, and detonators.

INVESTMENT, SIZE, PERSONNEL & MODERNIZATION: Replacement value is estimated at $456 million. There are 8.3 million square feet of covered facilities with 4 percent devoted to industrial production and the balance to storage. There are approximately 235 square miles of property. Current personnel strength is 71 Government and 571 contractor. Mobilization employment is projected at 1,900 personnel.

HISTORY: As a result of the catastrophic 1926 explosion at Lake Denmark, NJ (now part of Picatinny Arsenal), a Court of Inquiry recommended the establishment of a centrally located strategic naval ammunition depot to serve the Pacific. Groundbreaking took place July 1928 and commissioning September 1930. From 1930 to 1939 the primary function was storage. Operations were expanded to include production of various types of ammunition such as rockets, mines, depth charges, bombs, and torpedoes. It had operated continuously as a depot since commissioning until transfer to the SMCA. Facility modernization from SMCA transfer until the end of FY82 amounts to $3.9 million.

c. HOLSTON ARMY AMMUNITION PLANT

INSTALLATION: Holston AAP, Kingsport, Tennessee.

OPERATOR: GOCO-Holston Defense Corporation (Subsidiary of Eastman Kodak Company).

MISSION/CAPABILITY: Manufactures explosives including Compositions A, B, C, RDX-HMX, Composition A–3 and B–3, and many other special explosive products for all Services, Department of Energy, and NASA applications. Present monthly production of all materials is 1,200,000 pounds, with Composition B amounting to 800,000 pounds. Peak production of 326,000,000 pounds was achieved in 1968.

INVESTMENT, SIZE, PERSONNEL & MODERNIZATION: Estimated replacement value is $1,038 million. There are 2,465,000 square feet of floor space with approximately 60 percent devoted to manufacturing. Current personnel strength is 35 Government and 1,021 contractor. Estimated mobilization personnel requirements are 1,200.

HISTORY: Construction was initiated 1 July 1042 and completed 15 March 1944. During WWII 6,854 contractor and 500 Government personnel produced millions of pounds of Composition B. The plant was in standby status from 1 May 1946 to 1 April 1949. It has been active since 1 April 1949 and has expanded to meet requirements of both the Korean and Vietnam eras. Peak Vietnam employment was 3,613 contractor and 52 Government personnel. From FY70 to FY82, over $31 million of modernized/expanded facilities have been constructed or committed.

d. INDIANA ARMY AMMUNITION PLANT

INSTALLATION: Indiana AAP, Charlestown, Indiana.

OPERATOR: GOCO—ICI Americas, Inc.

MISSION/CAPABILITY: Loads, assembles, and packs propellant charges; manufactures single-base propellant and propellant charge bags and liners. Constitutes the only US capability for the manufacture of black powder.

INVESTMENT, SIZE, PERSONNEL & MODERNIZATION. Estimated replacement is $1,338 million. There are over 4.5 million square feet of facilities with about half devoted to production and about a third to supply. There are 10,649 acres of land. Current personnel strength is 42 Government and 1,611 contractor. Estimated mobilization personnel requirements are 20,300.

HISTORY: Construction was initiated for smokeless powder in August 1940 and completed May 1942. These facilities employed 27,154 at peak WWII production and exceeded the total WWI output of all US plants. After reactivation of Korea requirements, major layaway was again initiated in 1954. Facilities for manufacture and loading of bags were started January 1941 and completed February 1942. This was the first of four US bag-loading facilities built in WWII. Production was terminated August 1945. Manufacturing operations were reestablished in the 1952 and 1957 timeframe and then continuously from December 1961. Peak Korean and Vietnam bag-loading and manufacturing employment was 8,067 and 19,000, respectively. From FY70 to FY82 over $103 million of modernized/expanded facilities have been constructed or are in-process.

e. IOWA ARMY AMMUNITION PLANT

INSTALLATION: Iowa AAP, Middletown, Iowa.

OPERATOR: GOCO—Mason & Hanger—Silas Mason Co., Inc.

MISSION/CAPABILITY: Loads, assembles, and packs 90mm through 8–in projectiles, including components such as primers, detonators, fuzes, and boosters; mortar rounds—81mm and larger including their explosive components; antitank and antipersonnel mines; warheads (TOW and DRAGON) and demolition charges.

INVESTMENT, SIZE, PERSONNEL & MODERNIZATION: Estimated replacement value is $915 million. There are facilities totaling over 4.2 million square feet about equally divided between production and supply. There are a total of 19,257 acres of land. Current personnel strength is 958 contractor and 50 Government. Estimated mobilization personnel requirements are 7,200.

HISTORY: Construction was initiated in January 1941 and completed February 1942. WWII production was suspended 14 August 1945, and on 6 January 1946 the plant was converted to a GOCO status with a standby Government employment of 227 employees. From June 1946 to January 1950 fertilizer was produced by a Government contractor using the nitrate area. Production was resumed 1 August 1949 and by January 1951 Government employment reached 1,245. In March 1951 Silas Mason Co. assumed full operational responsibility. Southeast Asia created a requirement for major acceleration of activity; however, starting in FY74 layaway of several major lines was initiated. From FY70 to FY82 over $58 million of modernized/expanded facilities have been constructed or are in-process.

f. KANSAS ARMY AMMUNITION PLANT

INSTALLATION: Kansas AAP, Parsons, Kansas.

OPERATOR: GOCO—Day and Zimmerman, Inc.

MISSION/CAPABILITY: Loads, assembles, and packs 81mm mortars, 155mm Improved Conventional Munitions, 105mm howitzer projectiles, and CBU and related primers and detonators. A modem inactive lead azide facility also exists.

INVESTMENT, SIZE, PERSONNEL & MODERNIZATION: Estimated replacement value is $326 million. There are facilities totaling over 2.2 million square feet about equally divided between production and supply uses. There are a total of 13,727 acres of land. Current personnel strength is 717 contractor and 28 Government. Estimated mobilization personnel requirements are 4,600.

HISTORY: Construction was initiated August 1941 and completed November 1942. WWII peak employment was over 7,600 personnel. Production was terminated August 1945, and KAAP remained in standby until reactivation for Korea from August 1950 to the mid–50's. Peak Korean employment was just over 6,000. The plant was in standby status again from 1957 to 1967. Production to support Southeast Asia was initiated starting September 1967. Starting in 1971 some fuze, primer, and CBU lines were placed in standby. From FY70 to FY82, $19 million of modernized facilities have been constructed or are in-process.

g. LAKE CITY ARMY AMMUNITION PLANT

INSTALLATION: Lake City AAP, Independence, Missouri.

OPERATOR: GOCO—Remington Arms Company.

MISSION/CAPABILITY: Metal parts production and load. assemble, and pack of small caliber ammunition; i.e., 5.56mm, 7.62mm, 20mm, 30mm, as well as .30 and .50 caliber. This AAP produces about 93 percent of present Army small arms requirements. A new Small Caliber Ammunition Modernization Program facility for 5.6mm ammo production is the world's most modern and automated high speed, small caliber ammunition production facility.

INVESTMENT, SIZE, PERSONNEL & MODERNIZATION. Replacement value is $518 million. There are facilities totaling nearly 3.2 million square feet with about two-thirds devoted to production and one-third to supply. There are 3,909 acres of land. Current personnel strength is 66 Government and 1,768 contractor. Estimated mobilization personnel requirements are 10,900.

HISTORY: Construction was initiated in December 1940. The first building was completed October 1941. WWII peak employment was 21,229 personnel. On 28 August 1945, manufacturing was terminated. The plant was maintained in standby status until December 1950 with equipment laid away in position. This proved beneficial in meeting Korean requirements earlier than planned. It has remained active and has taken on small arms industrial engineering, surveillance, test, and technology missions. Since reactivation in 1950 over 25 billion rounds of accepted ammunition have been produced. From FY70 to FY82, over $103 million of modernized/expanded facilities have been constructed or are in-process.

h. LONE STAR ARMY AMMUNITION PLANT

INSTALLATION: Lone Star AAP, Texarkana, Texas.

OPERATOR: GOCO—Day and Zimmerman, Inc.

MISSION/CAPABILITY: Loads, assembles, and packs a variety of items including 60mm and 81mm mortars, hand grenades, 105mm howitzer, 155mm and 8–inch artillery rounds, rockets, and related fuzes, boosters, delays, primers, bursters, and detonators. Of the 13 major lines, six are in operation producing approximately 25 items, with the other in standby.

INVESTMENT, SIZE, PERSONNEL & MODERNIZATION: Estimated replacement value is $483 million. There are facilities totaling over 3 million square feet divided roughly between supply and production. There are 15,546 acres of land. Current personnel strength is 1,382 contractor and 69 Government. Estimated mobilization personnel requirements are 11,000.

HISTORY: Construction was initiated mid–1941 and completed the summer of 1942. Twelve production lines were in operation during WWII until completion of hostilities. From early 1946, as part of Red River Arsenal, work remained at a low level with many lines inactive, until the start of Korean hostilities. A total of ten lines was placed in production for support of Korea; after Korea production was again curtailed. Starting in 1961, and continuing for the duration of Southeast Asia hostilities, requirements dictated production increases to the point where all 13 lines were active. In December 1969 employment reached a peak of 11,463 personnel. From FY70 to FY82 over $93 million of modernized/expanded facilities have been constructed or are in-process.

i. LONGHORN ARMY AMMUNITION PLANT

INSTALLATION: Longhorn AAP, Marshall, Texas.

OPERATOR: GOCO—Thiokol Corporation.

MISSION/CAPABILITY: Load, assemble, and pack of illumination ammunition for artillery and mortars, pyrotechnics, grenade and ground signals, and rocket motors. Manufactures composite propellants for rockets and missiles.

INVESTMENT, SIZE, PERSONNEL & MODERNIZATION: Estimated replacement value was $207 million. There are facilities totaling over 1.35 million square feet with about one-third devoted to production and one-third to supply. There are 8,492 acres of land. Current personnel strength is 66 Government and 1,307 contractor. Mobilization personnel requirements are estimated at 2,500.

HISTORY: Construction started in 1942. Longhorn was primarily a producer of TNT during WWII having produced a war total of 393,000,000 pounds with a peak employment of 1,518 persons. Between 1945 and 1952, the installation was in standby status. From 1952 to 1956, rehabilitated facilities were used to load, assemble, and pack pyrotechnic ammunition with a peak of 530 employees. Facilities were placed in standby from 1956 to April 1963. In 1955 Thiokol Chemical Corporation began a pilot line operation for solid rocket motor propellants. Operations on pyrotechnic ammunition resumed in April 1963. From FY70 to FY82, over $13 million of modernized/expanded facilities have been constructed or are in-process.

j. LOUISIANA ARMY AMMUNITION PLANT

INSTALLATION: Louisiana AAP, Shreveport, Louisiana.

OPERATOR: GOCO—Thiokol Corporation.

MISSION/CAPABILITY: Loads, assembles, and packs 155mm projectiles, demolition charges, mines, rockets, and rocket warheads and related boosters, fuzes, and detonators. There is also a 155mm metal parts manufacturing facility.

INVESTMENT, SIZE, PERSONNEL & MODERNIZATION. The replacement value is $605 million. There are 2.8 million square feet of facilities, about 50 percent being for production and maintenance. There are 14,974 acres of land. Current employment is 32 Government and 863 contractor. Estimated mobilization personnel requirements are 4,100.

HISTORY: Construction was initiated in 1941. By May 1942 eight load lines were completed and operating. The plant was placed in standby status from 1945 to 1951. In 1958 a metal parts capability was established for the 155mm. After involvement with Korea requirements, the plant was again placed in standby from 1958 to September 1961. In September 1961 production was initiated to support Southeast Asia in traditional roles as well as for 155mm improved conventional munitions. From FY70 to FY82, over $81 million of modernized/expanded facilities have been constructed or are in-process.

k. McALESTER ARMY AMMUNITION PLANT

INSTALLATION: McALESTER AAP, McAlester, Oklahoma.

OPERATOR: GOGO—ARRCOM (formerly Navy).

MISSION/CAPABILITY: Load, assemble, and pack of 20 through 40mm, Navy Gun Ammunition, bombs, APAM (antipersonnel and materiel) CBU 59, rockets (including 2.75 inch), and propelling charges.

INVESTMENT, SIZE, PERSONNEL & MODERNIZATION: Replacement value is estimated at $530 million. There are more than 8 million square feet of covered facilities with 11% devoted to industrial production and the balance to storage facilities. There are 44,960 acres of land. Current personnel strength is 43 Government and 680 contractor. Mobilization employment is projected at 3,800.

HISTORY: Formerly (until 1977) an inland Naval Ammunition Depot providing backup to tidewater facilities, McAlester was commissioned May 1943 and completed December 1943. Additional buildings for producing and storing 20mm to 40mm medium and major caliber ammunition were constructed in 1946. McAlester had operated continuously as depot from commissioning until transfer to SMCA.

l. MILAN ARMY AMMUNITION PLANT

INSTALLATION: Milan AAP, Milan, Tennessee.

OPERATOR: GOCO—Martin Marietta Aluminum Sales, Inc.

MISSION/CAPABILITY: Loads, assembles, and packs 40mm grenades, 60 and 81mm mortars, 106mm recoilless and 105mm tank projectiles, cluster bomb units, mines, and related fuzes, primers, delay plungers, and boosters. A shell metal parts capability also exists.

INVESTMENT, SIZE, PERSONNEL & MODERNIZATION: Estimated replacement value is $535 million. There is a total of 3.7 million square feet of facilities with more than two-thirds devoted to supply and one-quarter to production. There are 22,543 acres of land. Current personnel strength is 804 Government. Estimated mobilization personnel requirements are 9,300.

HISTORY: Construction began January 1941 and was completed in January 1942. There were initially two separate plants, Wolf Creek Ordnance Plant and Milan Ordnance Depot. During WWII, peak employment reached 11,000; during Korea—8,000; during Vietnam—7,000. Milan Arsenal was created on 30 October 1945 and facilities were used primarily for receipt, storage, and processing of returned ammunition. In October 1957 the arsenal was placed in an inactive status. This lasted until January 1960. Milan Ordnance Plant was created from the industrial part of the Arsenal in November 1961. Since Vietnam, several lines were placed in layaway status. From FY70 to FY82, over $53 million in modernized/expanded facilities have been constructed or are in-process.

m. PINE BLUFF ARSENAL

INSTALLATION: Pine Bluff Arsenal, Pine Bluff , Arkansas.

OPERATOR: GOGO—ARRCOM

MISSION/CAPABILITY: Loads, assembles, and packs white phosphorus and smoke medium and major caliber artillery rounds, grenades, and rockets. Produces white phosphorus and smoke filler material. Fabricates chemical defensive material. Has chemical ammunition mission.

INVESTMENT, SIZE, PERSONNEL & MODERNIZATION. Estimated replacement value, including chemical facilities, is $634 million. Current personnel strength is 977 with 5,800 estimated under mobilization conditions. From

FY70 to FY82, over $30 million in modernization/expanded facilities have been constructed or are in-progress.

n. RADFORD ARMY AMMUNITION PLANT

INSTALLATION: Radford AAP, Radford, Virginia.

OPERATOR: GOCO—Hercules Inc.

MISSION/CAPABILITY: Manufactures single- double-, and triple-base propellants, rocket grains, and TNT.

INVESTMENT, SIZE, PERSONNEL & MODERNIZATION: Estimated replacement value is $702 million. There are over 3.4 million square feet of facilities with about 50 percent devoted to manufacture and production. There are 6,995 acres of land. Current personnel strength is 62 Government and 3,130 contractor. Mobilization employment is estimated at 9,100.

HISTORY: Construction began in September 1940, and production was initiated April 1941. During WWII it produced 500,000 pounds of smokeless powder and 1,000,000 pounds of pentalite per day. The plant was placed in a standby status at the end of WWII. In 1949 limited scale operations were resumed, and major rehabilitation of facilities took place including establishing missile propellant facilities. Because of high Southeast Asia requirements, employment peaked at 9,100 personnel in February 1969. Major modernization was begun in FY70 and approximately $254 million worth of facilities have been built or are in-process.

o. RIVERBANK ARMY AMMUNITION PLANT

INSTALLATION: Riverbank AAP, Riverbank, California.

OPERATOR: GOCO—Norris Industries, Inc.

MISSION/CAPABILITY: Manufactures metal parts for ICM grenades, 60mm and 81mm mortars, projectiles, and 105mm cartridge cases.

INVESTMENT, SIZE, PERSONNEL & MODERNIZATION: Estimated replacement value is $231 million. There are 792,500 square feet on 172 acres, most of which is devoted to industrial production. Current personnel strength is 8 Government and 69 contractor, with mobilization employment estimated at 2,500.

HISTORY: Built during WWI as an aluminum plant, Riverbank started its first ammunition production in 1952 in support of Korea. Production diminished until 1958 at which time the plant was laid away. In late 1966, the plant again was producing in support of Southeast Asia. The plant was again placed in standby in June 1976 and subsequently reactivated in 1978 for grenade production. From FY70 to FY82, over $14 million of modernized/expanded facilities have been constructed or are in-process.

p. SCRANTON ARMY AMMUNITION PLANT

INSTALLATION: Scranton AAP, Scranton, Pennsylvania.

OPERATOR: GOCO—Chamberlain Manufacturing Corporation.

MISSION/CAPABILITY: Manufactures metal parts for 155mm, 8-inch, and 175mm artillery munitions.

INVESTMENT, SIZE, PERSONNEL & MODERNIZATION. Estimated replacement value is $192 million. There are four major production buildings and one five-story administrative building on 15.3 acres. Current personnel strength is 22 Government and 480 contractor personnel employed. Mobilization employment is estimated at 2,040.

HISTORY: In 1952 DL&W Railroad shops were rehabilitated to meet shell metal parts requirements for the Korean emergency. The plant operated from December 1953 through March of 1963, at which time all contracts were terminated due to a labor dispute. Production was started again under the present contractor on 13 June 1963. The plant provided a high level of support to Southeast Asia requirements. From FY70 to FY82, over $49 million of modernized expanded facilities have been constructed or are in-process.

C-3. Inactive facilities.
a. Badger Army Ammunition Plant.

INSTALLATION: Badger AAP, Baraboo, Wisconsin.

OPERATOR: GOCO—Olin Corporation.

MISSION/CAPABILITY: Manufactures single- and double-base propellants, rocket propellant, and rocket grains.

INVESTMENT, SIZE, PERSONNEL & MOBILIZATION: Estimated replacement value is $760 million. There are 4.3 million square feet of facilities with about three-quarters devoted to manufacturing. There are 7,417 acres of land. Current standby employment is 7 Government and 341 contractor. Estimated mobilization employment is 8,750.

HISTORY: Construction was started in early 1942 and the plant produced millions of pounds of smokeless power, double-base rocket propellant, and E.C. powder during WWII. The plant remained in standby from 1945 to 1951. Reactivated in 1951, production totaled 286 million pounds in support of Korea. From 1958 to 1965 the plant again went into standby. Once again reactivated in 1965, the plant produced 446 million pounds in support of Southeast Asia. Since June 1975, the plant has been maintained in a standby status. From FY70 to FY82, over $55 million of modernization/expanded facilities have been constructed or are in-process.

b. Cornhusker Army Ammunition Plant.

INSTALLATION: Cornhusker AAP, Grand Island, Nebraska.

OPERATOR: GOCO—Mason and Hanger—Silas Mason Co., Inc.

MISSION/CAPABILITY: Loads, assembles, and packs major caliber ammunition, bombs, mines, and components.

INVESTMENT, SIZE, PERSONNEL, & MOBILIZATION: Estimated replacement value is $231 million. There are approximately 2.0 million square feet of facilities with about 60 percent devoted to manufacturing. There are 11,963 acres of land. Current standby employment is 4 Government and 81 contractor, with 3,000 estimated for mobilization.

HISTORY: Construction was started in March 1942. Initial production started November 1942 and continued for WWII. From late 1945 to February 1950, the plant was in standby. It was reactivated between April 1950 and early 1956, when it reverted to a layaway status. It was reactivated in September 1965 for Vietnam requirements. Peak employment during Vietnam was 5,169. By September 1974 all production facilities were again laid away. From FY70 to FY82 over $.2 million of modernized/expanded facilities have been constructed or are in-process.

c. Gateway Army Ammunition Plant.

INSTALLATION: Gateway AAP, St. Louis, Missouri.

OPERATOR: GOCO—Voss Machinery Co.

MISSION/CAPABILITY: Manufactures metal parts for major caliber ammunition.

INVESTMENT, SIZE, PERSONNEL & MODERNIZATION: Estimated replacement value is $118 million. There are 382,000 square feet of facilities with 288,000 square feet directly related to manufacturing. There are 14.9 acres of land; current employment consists of 15 contractor, with mobilization personnel estimated to be 745. This facility is currently in the process of being excessed.

HISTORY: Construction started in late 1942 with initial production beginning August 1943. It was used during WWII to produce heavy armor castings. During Korea, the plant produced medium tank armor castings. The facility was placed in layaway in 1954 and was idle from 1962 to 1967. Production of 175mm shell metal parts was initiated in December 1968 after an extensive rehabilitation program. The plant was laid away in a high readiness state on 30 September 1971. The plant has been declared excess to Army mobilization requirements, and disposal action was initiated in February 1980.

d. Hays Army Ammunition Plant.

INSTALLATION: Hays AAP, Pittsburgh, Pennsylvania.

OPERATOR: GOCO—Plant Facilities and Engineering, Inc.

MISSION/CAPABILITY: Manufactures metal parts for 105mm shell. Only Army plant having cold extrusion capability.

INVESTMENT, SIZE, PERSONNEL, & MODERNIZATION: Estimated replacement value is $69 million. The main plant is a building measuring 180 feet by 1,170 feet. There are 7.9 acres of land. Present standby employment is 11 contractor personnel, with mobilization requirements estimated at 1,650.

HISTORY: Built originally in 1942 for the Navy, Hays produced metal parts for 16–inch shells and also 5–inch breechblocks. The plant was transferred from the Navy to the Army in December 1966 and produced 250,000 105mm shells per month during 1968. Manufacture was concluded in May 1970, and layaway was completed in June 1971.

e. Joliet Army Ammunition Plant.

INSTALLATION: Joliet AAP, Joliet, Illinois.

OPERATOR: GOCO—Uniroyal, Inc.

MISSION/CAPABILITY: Loads, assembles, and packs medium and large caliber artillery ammunition and its components. Manufactures explosives such as TNT, TETRYL, and DNT.

INVESTMENT, SIZE, PERSONNEL, & MODERNIZATION: Estimated replacement value is $1,305 million. There are 1,496 buildings with 5.2 million square feet. About 25 percent of the square footage is devoted to manufacturing and 50% to supply. There are 23,543 acres of land. Current standby employment is 10 Government and 321 contractor, with mobilization employment estimated at 8,800.

HISTORY: A consolidation of Kankakee Ordnance Works and the Elwood Ordnance Plant, Joliet's construction was started in 1940. It was one of the largest producers of munitions during WWII. It was placed in standby status from 1945 until the Korean emergency. After rehabilitation and production in support of Korea, production from 1955 to 1965 was at a severely curtailed level with Elwood being put in standby in July 1965. Major reactivation occurred in 1966 to support Southeast Asia. From FY70 to FY82, over $104 million of modernized/expanded facilities have been constructed or are in-process.

f. Newport Army Ammunition Plant.

INSTALLATION: Newport AAP, Newport, Indiana.

OPERATOR: GOCO—Uniroyal Inc.

MISSION/CAPABILITY: Manufactures TNT. Has a major chemical agent capability.

INVESTMENT, SIZE, PERSONNEL & MODERNIZATION: Estimated replacement value is $310 million. There are over 1.5 million square feet of facilities with about one-third each devoted to production and storage facilities. There are 8,322 acres of land. Current standby employment is 8 Government and 292 contractor, with mobilization employment estimated to be 600.

HISTORY: Constructed as the Wabash River Ordnance Works in 1942, the plant produced extensive amounts of various explosives during WWII. The plant was laid away from 1946 to 1951. It was reactivated and again produced substantially for Korea. From 1957 to 1973, except for support of the chemical munition program, facilities were mostly inactive. In May 1973 modernized TNT lines began producing and continued through April 1974. TNT facilities were laid away in July 1975. Since FY70 no modernized/expanded facilities have been constructed or are in-process.

g. Ravenna Army Ammunition Plant.

INSTALLATION: Ravenna AAP, Ravenna, Ohio.

OPERATOR: GOCO-Ravenna Arsenal Inc. (Subsidiary of Firestone Tire & Rubber Company).

MISSION/CAPABILITY: Loads, assembles, and packs 155mm, 8–inch and 175mm projectiles, 4.2–inch mortars, and associated fuzes and primers. Excellent temperature/humidity-controlled storage facilities exist for industrial production equipment (IPE).

INVESTMENT, SIZE, PERSONNEL & MODERNIZATION: Estimated replacement value is $920 million. There are 5.4 million square feet of covered facilities with about one-third devoted to industrial and two-thirds to storage uses. These are 21,419 acres. Current employment is 4 Government and 165 contractor with mobilization employment estimated at 5,200.

HISTORY: Constructed in 1941, the Portage Ordnance Depot and Ravenna Ordnance Plant produced major caliber ammunition in support of WWII. From 1945 to 1950, production activities were devoted to renovation and demilitarization. The plant produced from 1950 to 1957, then was placed in inactive status until 1961. From 1961 the plant was used for demilitarization of large bombs and shells. From 1968 to 1972 the plant produced grenades and shells in support of Southeast Asia. It has been in layaway status since June 1972. From FY70 to FY82 over $3.7 million of modernized/expanded facilities have been constructed or are in-process.

h. St. Louis Army Ammunition Plant.

INSTALLATION: St. Louis AAP, St. Louis, Missouri.

OPERATION: GOCO—Donovan Construction Company.

MISSION/CAPABILITY: Manufactures metal parts for medium caliber projectiles.

INVESTMENT, SIZE, PERSONNEL & MODERNIZATION: Estimated replacement value is $174 million. There are 450,000 feet of industrial plant facilities on 21.05 acres. Current employment consists of 4 Government and 15 contractor employees, with mobilization employment estimated at 2,500.

HISTORY: Construction began January 1941 and production was started in December 1941. The facilities operated during WWII and the Korean emergency. It was in standby from 1945 to 1951 and again from May 1954 to September 1966. The plant has been in layaway status since April 1970. From FY70 to FY82 under $1.0 million of modernized/expanded facilities have been constructed.

i. Sunflower Army Ammunition Plant.

INSTALLATION: Sunflower AAP, DeSoto, Kansas.

OPERATOR: GOCO—Hercules Inc.

MISSION/CAPABILITY: Manufactures single-, double-, and triple-base propellants, rocket propellant, and rocket grains. Has the only Nitroguanidine manufacturing capability in the US.

INVESTMENT, SIZE, PERSONNEL & MODERNIZATION: Estimated replacement value is $883 million. There are 3.8 million square feet of facilities with about 65 percent devoted to manufacturing. There are 9,544 acres of land. Current standby employment is 9 Government and 583 contractor, with mobilization employment estimated at 6,500.

HISTORY: Construction was started in May 1942, and production of smokeless powder began 23 March 1943. During WWII, peak employment was 12,067, and over 200 million pounds of powder was produced. In July 1948, standby commenced and lasted until January 1951. Over 165 million pounds of powder was produced in support of Korea from January 1951 until May 1960, with a peak employment of 5,374. The plant was placed in standby from May 1960 until 20 August 1965, when it was reactivated for a 6-year period to support Southeast Asia. From FY70 to FY82, over $178 million of modernized/expanded facilities, including the nitroguanidine plant, have been constructed or committed.

j. Twin Cities Army Ammunition Plant.

INSTALLATION: Twin Cities AAP, New Brighton, Minnesota.

OPERATOR: GOCO—Donovan Construction Company and Federal Cartridge Company (Small Arms).

MISSION/CAPABILITY: Loads, assembles, and packs small caliber ammunition such as 5.56mm and 7.62mm. Also manufactures metal parts for 155mm shells.

INVESTMENT, SIZE, PERSONNEL & MODERNIZATION: Estimated replacement value is $587 million. There are 4.4 million square feet with almost 80 percent devoted to industrial production. There are 2,370 acres of land. Current standby employment is 7 Government and 128 contractor personnel, with mobilization employment estimated at 6,000.

HISTORY: Construction started in August 1941, and production began in February 1942. More than 4 billion rounds were produced during WWII. After WWII the plant was used for repack and demilitarization while in standby. Between August 1950 and December 1957, another 3.6 billion rounds of small arms were produced as well as 205 and 155mm shell metal parts. From August 1958 to December 1965, the plant was in standby status. Immediate reactivation was accomplished in December 1965 and from September 1966 to September 1973 almost 9 billion rounds were produced. The plant has been in layaway since October 1974 except for some shell metal parts production lines. From FY70 to FY82, over $18 million of modernized facilities have been constructed and committed.

k. Volunteer Army Ammunition Plant.

INSTALLATION: Volunteer AAP, Chattanooga, Tennessee.

OPERATOR: GOCO—ICI Americas, Inc.

MISSION/CAPABILITY: Manufactures TNT.

INVESTMENT, SIZE, PERSONNEL & MODERNIZATION: Estimated replacement value is $310 million. There are 1.1 million square feet of facilities with about 25 percent devoted to manufacturing, 40 percent to storage, and 20 percent to utilities. There are 7,300 acres of land. Current standby employment is 5 Government and 148 contractor, with mobilization employment estimated at 2,430.

HISTORY: Construction began in late 1941, and production started in July 1942. During WWII, 823 million pounds of TNT were produced. The plant was inactive between late 1945 and early 1952. During the period 1953 to 1957, another 283 million pounds were produced. The plant was inactive again between 1957 and 1966. It was reactivated on 29 April 1966 and operated continuously through March 1977. Since its inception, it has produced 1,765 million pounds of TNT. From FY70 to FY82, over $72 million of modernized facilities have been constructed or committed.

Glossary

Section I
Abbreviations

AAA
Army Ammunition Activity

AAE
Army Acquisition Executive

AAH
Advanced Attack Helicopter

AAIP
Army Ammunition Interoperability

AAO
Army Acquisition Objective

AAP
Army Ammunition Plan

AAP
Army Ammunition Plant

ABCA
America, Britain, Canada, Australia

ACR
Ammunition Condition Report

ADAM
Area Denial Artillery Munition

ADEN
Armament Development, Enfield

ADO
Army Distribution Objective

ADPE
Automatic Data Processing Equipment

AG
Army Guidance

AIF
Army Industrial Fund

AIRMS
Armament Industrial Readiness Management System

AITF
Ammunition Initiatives Task Force

AMDF
Army Master Data File

AMP
Army Materiel Plan

AMRAD
Armaments Munitions Requirements and Developments Committee

AMS–K
Ammunition Management System—Korea

APAM
Antipersonnel and Materiel

APC
Armored Personnel Carrier

APM
Army Program Memorandum

APE
Ammunition-Peculiar Equipment

AR
Army Regulation

ARNG
Army National Guard

ARRADCOM
US Army Armament Research and Development Command

ARRCOM
US Army Armament Materiel Readiness Command

ARSTAF
Army Staff

ASA(IL&FM)
Assistant Secretary of the Army (Installations, Logistics, and Financial Management)

ASA(RDA)
Assistant Secretary of the Army (Research, Development, and Acquisition)

ASARC
Army Systems Acquisitions Review Council

ASDA
Accountable Supply Distribution Activity

ASF
Army Stock Fund

ASP
Ammunition Supply Point

ASR
Available Supply Rate

BCS
Battery Computer System

BE
Belgium

BE
Base Ejection

BENELUX
Belgium, Netherlands, Luxembourg

BLSA
Basic Load Storage Area

BOIP
Basis of Issue Plan

CA
Canada

CA
Commercial Activities

CAA
US Army Concepts Analysis Agency

CALS
Committee for Ammunition Logistics Support

CARDS
Catalog of Approved Requirements Documents

CARES
Conventional Ammunition Readiness Evaluation System

CASPR
Conventional Ammunition Special Review

CBU
Cluster Bomb Unit

CG
Commanding General

CINCUSAREUR
Commander in Chief, US Army Europe

CLGP
Cannon-Launched Guided Projectile

CNAD
Conference of National Armament Directors

COCO
Contractor-Owned, Contractor-Operated

COE
Chief of Engineers

CONUS
Continental United States

COSIS
Care of Supplies in Storage

CSA
Chief of Staff, US Army

CSM
Chief of Staff Memorandum

CSR
Chief of Staff Regulation

CSR
Controlled Supply Rate

CTA
Common Table of Allowances

CTP
Coordinated Test Program

DALO–PL
ODCSLOG, Director of Plans, Readiness, and Systems

DALO–RM
ODCSLOG, Director of Resources and Management

DALO–SM
ODCSLOG, Director of Supply and Maintenance

DALO–TS
ODCSLOG, Director of Transportation, Energy, and Troop Support

DAMA–CSM
ODCSRDA, Munitions Division

DAMA–PPM
ODCSRDA, Policy, Plans and Management Division

DAMA–PPP
ODCSRDA, Procurement Programs and Budget Division

DAMA–PPR
ODCSRDA, RDTE Programs and Budget Division

DAMMS
Department of the Army Management Movement System

DAMO–FD
ODCSOPS, Force Management Directorate

DAMO–OD
ODCSOPS, Operations Readiness and Mobilization Directorate

DAMO–RQ
ODCSOPS, Requirements Directorate

DAMO–SS
ODCSOPS, Strategy, Plans and Policy Directorate

DAMPL
Director of the Army Master Priority List

DAPPL
Director of the Army Program Priority List

DARCOM
US Army Materiel Development and Readiness Command

DCP
Decision Coordinating Paper

DCSLOG
Deputy Chief of Staff for Logistics

DCSOPS
Deputy Chief of Staff for Operations and Plans

DCSRDA
Deputy Chief of Staff for Research, Development, and Acquisition

DDESB
DOD Explosives Safety Board

DEFA
Direction d'Etudes et Fabrication d'Armament

DESCOM
US Army Depot System Command

DIVAD
Division Air Defense (Gun) System

DOD
Department of Defense

DODAC
Department of Defense Ammunition Code

DODIC
DOD Identification Code

DP
Dual Purpose

DPM
Defense Program Memorandum

DSARC
Defense Systems Acquisition Review Council

DSU
Direct Support Unit

DT
Development Testing

DU
Depleted Uranium

ED
Engineering Development

EDCA
Executive Director for Conventional Ammunition

EOD
Explosive Ordnance Disposal

EPA
Extended Planning Institute

ET
Electronic Time (Fuze)

EUSA
US Eighth Army

FADAC
Field Artillery Digital Automatic Computer

FAE
Fuel Air Explosive

FASCAM
Family of Scatterable Mines

FCZ
Forward Communications Zone

FH
Field Howitzer (FRG)

FISO
Force Integration Staff Officer

FMS
Foreign Military Sales

FORSCOM
US Army Forces Command

FR
France

FRG
Federal Republic of Germany (now GE)

FSTS
Forward Storage Site

FY
Fiscal Year

FYPD
Five-Year Defense Program

FYTP
Five-Year Test Program

GE
Federal Republic of Germany

GEMSS
Ground-Emplaced Mine Scattering System

GMLR
Guided Missiles and Large Rockets (now MLRS)

GOCO
Government-Owned, Contractor-Operated

GOGO
Government-Owned, Government-Operated

GS
General Support

GSU
General Support Unit

HE
High Explosives

HEAT
High Explosives Antitank

HEP
High Explosive Plastic

HERA
High Explosive Rocket-Assisted

HEI
High Explosive Incendiary

HMX
High Melt Explosive

HQDA
Headquarters, Department of the Army

ICM
Improved Conventional Munitions

ILS
Integrated Logistic Support

IOC
Initial Operational Capability

IPE
Industrial Plant Equipment

IPF
Initial Production Facilities

IPP
Industrial Preparedness Program

IPR
In-Process Review

IWARS
Installation Worldwide Ammunition Reporting System

JCAP
Joint Conventional Ammunition Program

JMSNS
Justification for Major System New Start

JOPP
Joint Operating Policies and Procedures

JSPD
Joint Strategic Planning Document

KAMS
Korean Ammunition Management System

KE
Kinetic Energy

LAP
Load, Assemble, and Pack

LAW
Light Antitank Weapon

LOGSACS
Logistics Structure and Composition System

LOA
Letter of Agreement

LOI
Letter of Instruction

LP
Limited Production

LR
Letter Requirements

LRIP
Low-Rate Initial Production

LWCMS
Lightweight Company Mortar System

MAC
Military Airlift Command

MACOM
Major Command

MAP
Mission Area Panel

MENS
Mission Element Need Statement

NAIP
NATO Ammunition Interoperabilty Plan

M&E
Modernization and Expansion

MCA
Military Construction Army

MFP
Materiel Fielding Plan

MICOM
US Army Missile Command

MILSTAMP
Military Standard Transportation and Movement Procedures

MILSTRIP
Military Standard Requisitioning and Issue Procedures

MIPR
Military Interdepartmental Purchase Request

MLRS
Multiple Launch Rocket System

MMC
Materiel Management Center

MMT
Manufacturing Methods and Technology

MO
Multi-Option

MOA
Memorandum of Agreement

MOPMS
Modular Pack Mine System

MOS
Military Occupational Specialty

MOU
Memorandum of Understanding

MPBMA
Munitions Production Base Modernization Agency

MP
Multipurpose

MPTS
Metal Parts

MS³
Munitions System Support Structure

MSC
Military Sealift Command

MSC
Major Subordinate Command

MTMC
Military Traffic Management Command

MTOE
Modification Table of Organization and Equipment

MTSQ
Mechanical Time Super Quick

MWARS
MACOM Worldwide Ammunition Reporting System

NAIP
NATO Ammunition Interoperability Plan

NATO
North Atlantic Treaty Organization

NDRF
National Defense Reserve Fleet

NETP
New Equipment Training Program

NGB
National Guard Bureau

NICP
National Inventory Control Board

NIIN
National Item Identification Number

NL
Netherlands

NOR
Norway

NSN
National Stock Number

OAP
Outline Acquisition Plan

O/C
Other Customer

OCSA
Office, Chief of Staff, US Army

ODCSLOG
Office, DCSLOG

ODCSOPS
Office, DCSOPS

ODCSPER
Office, DCSPER

ODCSRDA
Office, DCSRDA

OMA
Operation and Maintenance, Army

OPA
Other Procurement, Army

OPLANS
Operations Plans

OSD
Office, Secretary of Defense

OT
Operational Test

OTEA
US Army Operational Test and Evaluation Agency

PAA
Procurement of Ammunition, Army

PA&ED
Program Analysis and Evaluation Directorate

P&E
Propellant and Explosives

PARR
Program Analysis and Resource Review

PGB
Program Budget Guidance

PBC
Program Budget Committee

PBP
Production Base Plan

PBY
Type of Explosive

PEP
Plant Equipment Package

PEPMIS
Plant Equipment Package Information System

PIN
Pallet Identification Number

PIP
Product Improvement Proposal

PM
Project Manager

POM
Program Objective Memorandum

POMCUS
Prepositioning of Materiel Configured to Unit Sets

PPBS
Planning, Programing, and Budgeting System

PWRMS
Prepositioned War Reserve Materiel Stocks

PSP
Prestock Point

QA
Quality Assurance

QAR
Quarterly Ammunition Review

QASAS
Quality Assurance Specialist (Ammunition Surveillance)

QRS
Quick Reaction Site

RA
Rocket-Assisted

RAMIT
Relocatable Ammunition Magazine In-Theater

RAP
Rocket-Assisted Projectile

RASP
Reserve Ammunition Supply Point

RCZ
Rear Combat Zone

RDAISA
Research, Development, and Acquisition Information Systems Agency

RDF
Rapid Deployment Force

RDTE
Research, Development, Test, and Evaluation

RDX
Research Department Explosive

REFORGER
Return of Forces to Germany

RF
Radio Frequency

ROC
Required Operational Capability

ROKA
Republic of Korea Army

RSI
Rationalization, Standardization, and Interoperability

RSR
Required Supply Rates

S&A
Safing and Army

S/A
Security Assistance

SAA
Small Arms Ammunition

SAAS
Standard Army Ammunition System

SACS
Structure and Composition System

SAG
Study Advisory Group

SAILS
Standard Army Intermediate Level Supply

SALS
Standard Army Logistics System

SALS—K
Single Ammunition Logistics System-Korea

SAMPAM
Systems for Automation of Materiel Plans for Army Material

SCS
Special Contingency Stockpile

SELCOM
Select Committee

SLUFAE
Surface-Launched Unit, Fuel Air Explosive

SMCA
Single Manager for Conventional Ammunition

SP
Self-Propelled

STANAG
Standardized Agreement

STOG
Science and Technology Objective Guide

STRAF
US Strategic Army Forces

SUMS
Standard USAREUR Munitions System

TAA
Total Army Analysis

TAAC
Training Ammunition Authorization Committee

TAADS
The Army Authorization Documents System

TACFIRE
Tactical Fire Direction System

TAG
The Adjutant General

TAMIS
Training Ammunition Management Information System

TAMS
Training Ammunition Management System

TDA
Tables of Distribution and Allowances

TDP
Technical Data Package

TECOM
US Army Test and Evaluation Command

TIWG
Test Integrated Working Group

TMDE
Test, Measurement, and Diagnostic Equipment

TOA
Total Obligational Authority

TOE
Tables of Organization and Equipment

TP
Target Practice

TPFDL
Time-Phased Force Deployment List

TRADOC
US Army Training and Doctrine Command

UIC
Unit Identification Code

UK
United Kingdom

USAEARA
US Army Equipment Authorizations Review Activity

USALEA
US Army Logistics Evaluation Agency

USAREUR
US Army Europe

USARJ
US Army Japan

USARPAC
US Army Pacific

USN
United States Navy

VCSA
Vice Chief of Staff, Army

VSS
Vessel Support System

VT
Variable Time

VTAADS
Vertical TAADS

WARF
Wartime Replacement Factor

WARRAMP
Wartime Requirements for Ammunition, Materiel, and Personnel

WESTCOM
US Army Western Command

WARS
Worldwide Ammunition Reporting System

WP
White Phosphorus

WRSA
War Reserve Stocks For Allies

Section II
Terms
This section contains no entries.

Section III
Special Abbreviations and Terms
This section contains no entries.

PIN 038787–000